ADOBE® PHOTOSHOP® CS4
HOW-TOs
100 ESSENTIAL TECHNIQUES

CHRIS ORWIG

Adobe Photoshop CS4 How-Tos
100 Essential Techniques

Chris Orwig

This Adobe Press book is published by
Peachpit.

For information on Adobe Press books, contact:

Peachpit
1249 Eighth Street
Berkeley, CA 94710
510/524-2178
510/524-2221 (fax)

Peachpit is a division of Pearson Education.
For the latest on Adobe Press books, go to www.adobepress.com
To report errors, please send a note to errata@peachpit.com

Project Editor: Susan Rimerman
Production Editor: Tracey Croom
Developmental Editor: Anne Marie Walker
Technical Editor: Sean McCormack
Proofreader: Suzie Nasol
Composition: ICC MacMillan Inc.
Indexer: FireCrystal Communications
Cover and Interior Design: Mimi Heft

ISBN-13: 978-0-321-57782-5

ISBN-10: 0-321-57782-5

9 8 7 6 5 4 3 2 1

Printed and bound in the United States of America

Dedication

To my Dad who gave me my first camera and who encouraged me to pursue my dreams—thanks!

Acknowledgments

Thanks to an amazing editorial and production team: Susan Rimerman, Anne Marie Walker, Sean McCormack, Suzie Nasol, and Tracey Croom—it has been a delight working with you.

Finally, a special thank you to my colleagues, the professional photography faculty at the Brooks Institute in Santa Barbara, California, for their boundless inspiration. And thanks to the administration for its tremendous support and ability to empower us to be the best and the brightest!

Contents

CHAPTER ONE

Getting Started

Adobe Photoshop CS4 is the essential tool for perfecting images. If you are an amateur or seasoned pro who is interested in learning how to create more communicative, compelling, and breathtaking images, this book is for you!

Adobe Photoshop CS4 How-Tos approaches Photoshop from a professional photographic perspective. In pro photography, the quality of an image is often defined by how it affects the viewer. Thus, all the techniques in this book are designed to help you create images with impact. My hope is that the 100 clear and concise tips that are presented in this book will catapult you to new creative heights.

In other words, this book is designed to help you quickly and easily acquire the technical skills that enable you to be more creative. As you become more familiar with it, you'll find it is packed with valuable techniques. If you're like me, you may be tempted to skip ahead to read about the techniques that are most pertinent to your own workflow. That approach works with this book, but be sure to read this chapter thoroughly, since it aims to provide a solid footing in Photoshop that can help as you apply what you've learned throughout the rest of the book. In particular, it discusses specifying color, settings, and preferences; customizing the interface; and more.

Let's get started!

#1 Managing Color

Have you ever edited an image in which the color looked good on your monitor but not as good in the final print? When this happens, it is such a let down. The solution is to implement a color managed workflow, which clarifies the communication between a monitor and printer, and ensures that your final prints will look their best.

In more technical terms, the goal of color management is to minimize the difference between color created via light (monitor) and color created via ink (printer), so that in the end the color is accurate. Of course, nothing is more gratifying than seeing a printed image in which the color is spot on!

You can specify color management settings in Photoshop using the Color Settings dialog box. To open the Color Settings choose Edit > Color or press Shift + Ctrl (Windows) Command (Mac) + K. The default Color Settings preset is North America General Purpose 2 (**Figure 1a**).

Figure 1a The default Color Settings preset, North American General Purpose 2, uses the sRGB color space.

For anyone who creates photographs, this setting is less desirable because it uses the sRGB color space. To make a long story short, this color space has a limited number of colors. While the number of colors is adequate for viewing images onscreen, it's inadequate for high-quality printing. Choose the North American Prepress 2 preset instead. It uses the Adobe RGB color space, which accurately handles a much wider range of color (**Figure 1b**). The end result is more colorful and vibrant photographs.

Figure 1b Switching to the North American Prepress 2 preset changes the working color space to Adobe RGB.

Tip
To help you create high-quality, color-managed prints, be sure to read Chapter 14, "Output." It covers the specifics for accurate color printing.

Note
If you are using Adobe Photoshop Lightroom, I recommend choosing Pro Photo RGB because it will help you take advantage of an even larger color space. If you're not using Lightroom, it will probably be best to stick with Adobe RGB (1998).

Monitor Calibration

Choosing the appropriate color settings in Photoshop is the first step toward creating a color managed workflow. The next step is to calibrate your monitor to create a monitor profile. By creating a profile you can further clarify the communication between your monitor and other output devices. For more information on monitor calibration and color management in general, visit color guru Jeff Schewe's Web site at http://photoshopnews.com and click on any of the Color Management section links.

#2 Modifying Preferences

You can customize Photoshop to suit your own way of working by changing various program options.

Choose Photoshop > Preferences (Mac) or Edit > Preferences (Windows) to open the Preferences dialog box. Because Photoshop provides many more options than can fit in a single dialog box, the options are grouped into categories, and each category is displayed on its own pane (General, Interface, File Handling, and so on). Click an item in the list on the left to switch to that pane. For the most part, the default settings will be fine, but a couple preferences are worth modifying.

Let's begin with the Image Interpolation setting on the General pane. When you resize an image or change its resolution, pixels are added or removed, and Photoshop has to recalculate the values of the new pixels. This calculation is called resampling. When Photoshop resamples an image, it has to calculate, or *interpolate,* the pixel values in the image. Photoshop can perform this calculation using one of several interpolation methods—which one it uses is up to you.

To designate which one you'd like to use, select General on the left of the Preferences dialog box, and then choose a setting from the Image Interpolation menu. In my case, because I tend to start with large Camera Raw, PSD, or JPEG files that I resize downward, I designate Bicubic Sharper as my default interpolation method. This setting applies to any operation that uses a tool that resizes the image, such as Crop, Free Transform, and so on (**Figure 2a**).

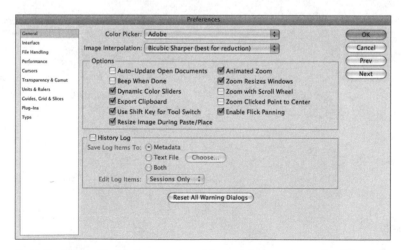

Figure 2a Choose Bicubic Sharper when sizing your images to a smaller dimension.

Note
If you find that you typically begin with smaller images and then enlarge them, be sure to choose the Bicubic Smoother setting as your interpolation method.

In addition, in the General options, I recommend that you select Animated Zoom and Enable Flick Panning to take advantage of these new features. Animated Zoom allows you to zoom with quick and fluid precision. Flick Panning allows you to navigate around your image with increased speed and ease.

Next, in the Interface pane (**Figure 2b**), you have the ability to modify the visuals that surround your document. Choose a Color and Border that best suits your personal preference. Keep in mind that typically it is best to keep the visuals that surround your documents simple so they are not distracting. For the border options choose Line, Drop Shadow, or None. In addition, be sure to select the option to Remember Panel Locations so Photoshop will remember (and not reset) your panels every time you open and close the application.

Figure 2b Choose a background color and document border for the three different screen modes.

Another preference you'll want to pay some attention to is located in the File Handling pane. In the File Compatibility area of that pane, deselect Ask Before Saving Layered TIFF Files. Why turn off this preference? Because when you save your work in Photoshop, most of the time you'll likely save it as a TIFF file, so you don't need Photoshop to ask you about saving the layers every time you save the document (unless of course you are a glutton for pain) (**Figure 2c**).

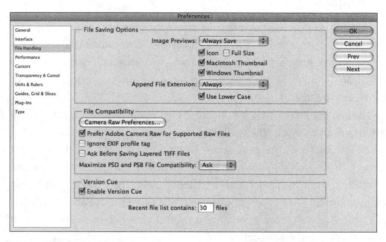

Figure 2c Deselect the Ask Before Saving Layered TIFF Files option to save time.

If the files you are working on will need to be opened in an older version of Photoshop or Adobe Photoshop Lightroom, you may want to select Always from the menu beside Maximize PSD and PSB File Compatibility. With this setting enabled, every time you save a layered file, a composite version of the image will be added to the file so that it can be opened by applications that don't support Photoshop layers.

The Performance pane provides access to controls that let you tailor Photoshop to the particulars of your hardware. Photoshop is a glutton for memory—the more you can give it, the happier it is and the more smoothly it runs. By default, Photoshop uses your computer's RAM—the fast, chip-based memory on the logic board. But if you have many images open at once or several large images with many layers, you may fill RAM to overflowing. In this case, Photoshop begins using empty space on your hard drive as memory; as a result, your computer's performance takes a nosedive because accessing a hard drive is much slower than accessing memory chips.

One way to avoid this problem is to make sure Photoshop has access to as much RAM as it needs. In the Memory Usage area of the Performance pane, drag the slider to the right to assign more RAM to Photoshop. If you run other programs at the same time as Photoshop (for example, if you listen to iTunes as you work), don't move the slider to 100%. Leave some RAM for those other applications (**Figure 2d**).

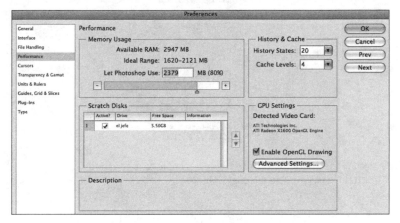

Figure 2d Improve performance by increasing the amount of RAM available to Photoshop.

The Type pane also contains some useful preferences. Select Type, and in the Font Preview Size menu, you'll discover that the Adobe development team has a great sense of humor, calling the larger font previews Extra Large and Huge (**Figure 2e**).

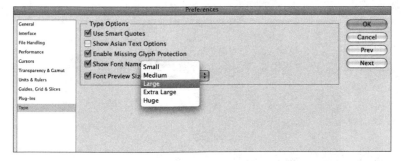

Figure 2e Change the Font Preview size to meet your workflow needs.

Open Bridge

In the previous version of Photoshop, the General pane contained the preference option to automatically launch Bridge every time you opened Photoshop. This preference has moved and been modified to be even better. Now you can launch Bridge every time you start your computer. You should select this option because you'll most likely use Bridge to access and open your files frequently. I'll mention this again in Chapter 3, "Using Adobe Bridge," but if you want to set this preference now, navigate to Bridge, open the preferences, and choose Advanced > Start Bridge at Login.

How big is huge, and where can you find this font preview? Select the Type tool (or press the T key) and open one of the Font menus in the options bar (**Figure 2f**).

Figure 2f The Font Preview size displays sample text at various sizes. In this case, the size selected is Huge.

#3 Introducing the Tools Panel

When you're working in Photoshop, you'll want to have the Tools panel open so you can easily make selections, type, paint, draw, retouch, and more. Because you will reach for the Tools panel frequently to switch tools, it's best to position it and configure it in a way that fits your particular workflow needs.

Positioning the Tools panel

If the Tools panel isn't displayed onscreen, choose Window > Tools. By default, the Tools panel is encased in a gray rectangle on the left edge of the screen called the dock. To position the Tools panel:

* Drag the panel by its title bar (the gray bar at the top) to remove it from the dock. The Tools panel will float free and can be positioned anywhere on the screen.

* Drag the panel to the far left to redock it (**Figure 3a**).

Docked   Floating

Figure 3a The Tools panel can be positioned either in the panel well or floating anywhere onscreen.

To configure the Tools panel, click the double arrows at the top of the Tools panel to switch between single-column and double-column format (**Figure 3b**).

Figure 3b Click the double arrows to display the tools in one or two columns.

Identifying tools

The Tools panel groups related tools together (**Figure 3c**). When viewing the Tools panel in a single column, notice that the first group of tools is used for selections, cropping, slices, and measuring. The second group of tools is great for retouching, painting, burning and dodging, and more. The third set of tools is used for drawing and type. In the last set of tools you'll find the 3D (Photoshop Extended) and navigation tools. If you move the cursor over a tool, a tool tip displays the name of the tool and its keyboard shortcut (**Figure 3d**).

Selection tools

Crop and Slice measuring

Retouching and Painting

Drawing and Type

3D and Navigation

Figure 3c Find the tool you need more quickly by understanding how the tools are grouped together.

Figure 3d Point at each tool with the mouse pointer to display a tool tip.

Selecting tools

To select a tool, click it. To use a tool that's hidden in a pop-up menu (indi-cated by a small triangle), click and hold on the tool. When the pop-up menu displays, select another tool (**Figure 3e**).

Figure 3e To display and select hidden tools, press and hold on a tool's icon.

The hidden tool replaces the original tool in the Tools panel.

To quickly switch tools, press the keyboard shortcut shown in each tool's tool tip. For example, you can press the V key to select the Move tool or press the T key to select the Type tool. (If the text input cursor is flashing, you cannot use the single-letter shortcuts. Finish typing, exit the text field, and then try the single-letter shortcuts.

Tool Selection Speed Tip

If you like speed tips, you'll get a lot out of this one. Here's the scoop: You can use the Shift key and the single letter shortcuts to cycle between the alternate tools. For example, press J to select the Spot Healing tool, and then press Shift + J to cycle through the Healing Brush, Patch, and Red Eye tools.

#4 Discovering the Application Bar

The Application bar (**Figure 4a**) is a welcomed new feature to the Creative Suite (Photoshop, Illustrator, InDesign, etc.). For starters it is helpful to note that the bar appears differently on a Mac and PC. You can find the Application bar just below the menu bar (Mac) or combined with the menu bar (PC). The first icon on the left is the Application icon. At first glance you might wonder why it is there. Well, you'll soon discover that the interface layout across the Creative Suite application is incredibly similar. This icon serves as a quick visual to let you know where you are. To the right of the Application icon is the Bridge icon, which acts like a button. Click the Bridge icon to open Bridge.

Figure 4a The Application bar allows you to access frequently needed layout and navigational options.

The next set of icons has a bit more functionality and options (**Figure 4b**). The View Extras icon allows you to Show/Hide Guides, Grids, and Rulers. The Zoom level gives you the ability to quickly change the document zoom to a specific level. To select a different zoom level, type in a percentage. Or press Ctrl (Windows) Command (Mac) and position the cursor over the percent; scrubby sliders will appear. Drag to the left or right to change the zoom. The Hand tool and Zoom tool icons provide you with another way, apart from the Tools panel, to select those tools.

Figure 4b Click an icon in the Application bar to access that feature, or if there is an arrow to the right of the icon, click and hold to reveal more options.

The Rotate View tool is new to CS4. It gives you the ability to view your documents at various angles without actually rotating the pixels. In other words, your documents are no longer locked into a vertical or horizontal orientation and can be viewed at any angle. Next, the Arrange Documents icon allows you to change the layout when you have multiple documents open at one time (**Figure 4c**). The Screen Mode icon (which was previously in the Toolbox in CS3) gives you the ability to select one of the different screen modes.

Figure 4c The majority of the Arrange Documents
menu is self-explanatory. Yet, it is helpful to note that
at the top of the menu you can select four different tile
arrangements. Underneath, choose among 16 arrangements
to display a specific number of document windows at one
time.

Tip
*Mac users can toggle the visibility of the Application bar by choosing
Window > Application Bar.*

#5 Using the Options Bar

The options bar appears below the menu and Application bar at the top of the workspace. Because the options bar is so useful, you'll want to keep it visible.

- When you first launch Photoshop, the options bar is docked at the top of the window.

- You can move the options bar in the workspace by using the gripper bar (the gray dotted bar on the far left), and you can dock it at the top or bottom of the screen.

- To open and close the options bar, choose Window > Options.

The options bar is context sensitive—it changes as you select different tools or different items in your document. Some settings in the options bar (such as painting modes and opacity) are common to several tools, and some are specific to one tool. Click any tool in the Tools panel to view the options. For example, when the Type tool is selected, the Type tool options are visible in the options bar (**Figure 5**).

Figure 5 When the Type tool is selected, the options bar lets you choose text-related parameters, such as font family, style, size, anti-aliasing, color, alignment, and more.

Tip
To reset a tool's options to their default settings, right-click (Windows) or Control-click (Mac) on the tool's icon in the options bar and choose Reset Tool. Choose Reset All to do the same for all tools at once.

When you want to focus only on the Tools panel and options bar, press Shift + Tab to hide the rest of the panels while keeping the Tools panel and options bar visible.

#6 Customizing the Interface

One of the most anticipated and celebrated new features in Photoshop CS4 is the updated user interface. It is streamlined, simplified, and customizable in ways that were previously unimaginable. (An added bonus is that Adobe has revamped the user interfaces of all the programs in Creative Suite 4 so that they're consistent in look and operation.) The intent of these new features is to provide the user with the ability to dedicate more screen real estate to the image without having to lose quick access to the tools and panels. At the same time, you can customize the interface to fit your particular needs.

By default, the Photoshop panels are gathered into groups and stacks, and stored in a dock on the right edge of the screen. Panels can be collapsed into icons to save space, and these icons can also be grouped, stacked, or docked. Drag any panel by its title bar (or panel icon) out of the dock to a new location. In this manner you can either have the panels "float" as they did in previous versions of Photoshop (CS2 and earlier), or you can group them or stack them with other panels to suit your working needs.

Panel docking

A dock is a vertical collection of panels or panel groups that are free floating or are attached to the left or right edge of the screen. Each dock is surrounded by a dark-gray rectangle. When dragging a panel or panel group into a dock, a blue rectangle appears when the panel is hovering over a *drop zone*. This line indicates that if you release the mouse, your panel will be added to the dock.

- To dock a panel, drag it by its tab into the dock or to the top, bottom, or in between other panels. When the blue drop zone appears, release the mouse button (**Figure 6a**).

Tab

Drop zone highlight

The Color panel being moved

The Color panel docked with the Adjustments and Masks Tab Group

Figure 6a A panel can be docked with other panel Tab Groups. At the top, the Color panel (that was originally docked with the Swatches and Styles panels) is being moved so that it can be docked with the Adjustments and Masks Tab Group. The Color tab was clicked and dragged over the destined Tab Group until a blue highlight appeared around the edge of the group. The end result is visible in the screen grab on the right.

- To dock a panel group, drag it by its title bar (the solid empty bar above the tabs) into the dock's drop zone and release.

- To remove a panel or panel group, drag it out of the dock by its tab or title bar. You can drag it into another dock or make it free floating.

Panel stacking

When you drag a panel out of its dock but not into a drop zone, the panel floats freely, allowing you to position it anywhere on the screen. Panels can also float in the workspace when first opened from the Window menu. You can stack free-floating panels or panel groups together so they move as a unit when you drag the topmost title bar. (Panels that are part of a dock cannot be stacked or moved as a unit in this way.)

To stack free-floating panels, drag a panel by its tab to the drop zone at the bottom of another panel (**Figure 6b**).

Separate panels

Panels stacked as a dock

Figure 6b On the left the Channels and Layers panels are free floating. On the right the panels have been stacked together and can thus be moved in unison.

To change the stacking order, drag a panel up or down by its tab.

Note

Be sure to release the tab over the narrow drop zone between panels rather than the broad drop zone in a title bar or else they will dock as discussed in the previous section.

To remove a panel or panel group from the stack so that it floats by itself, drag it out by its tab or title bar.

Panel icons

Docked panels are displayed full size by default. Click the double-arrow icon at the top of the dock to expand or collapse the panels that are in the dock into a set of icons (**Figure 6c**).

Essentials (Default)
Workspace layout

Essentials panels
collapsed to icons

Figure 6c On the left are the default Essentials Workspace panels. On the right those same panels have been collapsed to icons.

By viewing the panels as icons, you can dedicate more screen space to the image. To use a collapsed panel, click its icon to expand it. Click the double-arrow icon to expand or collapse all the panels in the dock.

Tip
To better see the labels of panels that have been collapsed to icons, drag the edge of the dock to the right to widen it. Or drag the edge of the dock to the left to conceal the icon labels.

Full Screen view mode

One of my photographic mentors (and heroes) is the acclaimed photographer Ralph Clevenger. When creating and working on photographs, Ralph is fond of repeating, "reduce and simplify." One way of following this mantra in regard to Photoshop is to reduce onscreen clutter by using different screen modes built into the program. The choices are as follows:

- **Standard Screen mode.** The default mode in which document windows, all panels, and the options bar are visible.

- **Maximized Screen mode.** The document window expands to fill the space between the docks.

(continued on next page)

Interface Tip

The Photoshop CS4 interface has been trimmed and slimmed. But you may still want to minimize it even further to focus in on your images. Use the following shortcuts to further simplify your workspace. Press Tab to hide everything except the document windows and menu bar (if it's visible). Press Tab again to make the panels and the options bar reappear. Or press Shift + Tab to hide/show the panels on the right.

Changing the User Interface Font Size

Photoshop CS4 is truly more customizable than any previous version of Photoshop. Now you can even change the size of the text in the panels and tool tips. To make this change, choose Photoshop > Preferences > Interface (Mac) or Edit > Preferences > Interface (Windows) to open the Interface Preferences. Then choose a size from the UI (User Interface) Font Size menu.

Panel Controls

To minimize a panel, panel group, or a stack of panels, click the Minimize button in its title bar.

Most panels have more options than can fit on the panel. You'll find these extra options and commands listed on the panel menu, which you open by clicking the icon 🔳 on the upper right of the panel.

- **Full Screen mode with Menu Bar.** The active document window fills the entire screen surrounded by 50% gray and no scroll bars.

- **Full Screen mode.** The active document is centered in a full-screen black background with no title bar, menu bar, or scroll bars.

You can cycle through these screen modes by clicking the Change Screen Mode button located in the Application bar (**Figure 6d**).

Figure 6d Clicking the Change Screen Mode button displays the three different screen modes.

#7 Choosing a Workspace

The new CS4 interface is clean, simple, refreshing, and customizable. However, if you are migrating to CS4 from a previous version of Photoshop, the new interface organization may throw you off. Not to worry. You can try out different layouts. From the Workspace menu on the Application bar (**Figure 7a**) or by selecting Window > Workspace, choose Workspace options.

Workspace button

Figure 7a Click the Workspace button located on the far right of the Application bar to select different workspace configurations.

If you want to highlight throughout Photoshop the menu items that are new or that have been added or modified in CS4, click the Workspace menu button in the Application bar and choose What's New in CS4 (**Figure 7b**).

Figure 7b Click the Workspace menu button in the Application bar and select What's New in CS4 to help you determine which are the new or improved features.

Help Is Close at Hand

In this first chapter, you have learned quite a bit, and as you can tell, Photoshop is a profoundly deep application. At times its depth can be overwhelming, even for the brightest of students. At the same time, help is always just a short click away. One of the most valuable built-in Help tools is the Adobe Help Viewer. To launch it, select Help > Photoshop Help. You can also visit Adobe TV at http://tv.adobe.com or http://www.adobe.com/ designcenter/video_ work shop to watch a handful of free instructional videos. For more in-depth video based training created by myself, you can visit http://www. lynda.com.

Then when you open any of the top pull-down menus, the options that have been updated, improved, or added to CS4 will be highlighted (**Figure 7c**).

Figure 7c As a result of choosing Window > Workspace > What's New in CS4, Color Range, Refine Edge, and Edit in Quick Mask Mode menu items in the Select menu are highlighted.

CHAPTER TWO

Working with Digital Image Files

It's never been a more exciting time for those of us who are interested in digital imaging. We are literally in the midst of a digital revolution, where new technological discoveries are spawning remarkable creativity, vitality, and growth. As a result, knowing how to work with digital files has never been more important.

This chapter is designed to function as a cornerstone to the rest of the work you do in Photoshop as you read through the book. It will get you up to speed on many of the fundamentals of digital imaging and show you how to open, save, and resize images, among other things.

#8 Opening and Viewing Multiple Documents

A few different methods are available for opening an image file into Photoshop. You can use Adobe Bridge, the powerful file browser application that ships with all the Creative Suite products (see Chapter 3, "Using Adobe Bridge"). If you'd rather stay within Photoshop, however, simply choose File > Open or press Ctrl + O (Windows) or Command + O (Mac) and navigate to the location where your image file(s) is stored. By default, you'll use your operating system's Open dialog box (**Figure 8a**).

Figure 8a The Open dialog box in Mac OS X.

In the Open dialog box you can choose to open one or more images. When you decide to open multiple images, new to Photoshop CS4 is the ability to open these files as tabs (**Figure 8b**). The feature is called tabbed document viewing, and it will revolutionize how you work with and navigate among multiple files. To view one of the images, simply click on the tab. In addition, you can rearrange the tab order by clicking on a tab and dragging it to a new position.

Currently selected tab

Figure 8b The tabbed document view allows you to see the titles of and then quickly access a document when you have multiple documents open at one time.

#9 Understanding the Document Window

In Photoshop, each open image can be displayed in its own document window. Crucial information about the image is displayed within the top and bottom edges of the window (**Figure 9a**).

Figure 9a The frame of the document window contains valuable information about the file displayed within.

At the top of the window, the filename is listed first (in this case, images_01.jpg). To the right of the filename is the zoom percentage, which is also displayed on the lower left of the window. At a zoom of 100%, each pixel in your image is represented by a pixel in your display. This is useful if you're preparing images for Web pages, because it shows you how large the image will appear in a Web browser. If you're working with higher-resolution images, the 100% zoom is helpful to see the actual pixels, although most of the time you'll probably want to use a smaller zoom percentage.

Tip

Right-click (Windows) Control-click (Mac) on the filename at the top of the window to reveal the folder hierarchy and see where the image is located (Figure 9a). In addition, after you have clicked on the filename you can navigate to any of the folders by selecting the folder name from the menu.

Returning to the top of the document window, you'll find the color space and bit depth in parentheses to the right of the zoom percentage. In this case, the color mode is RGB and the bit depth is 8 bits per channel. To change the color space and/or bit depth, choose your options by selecting Image > Mode (**Figure 9b**).

Figure 9b Choose Image > Mode to change the color mode and/or bit depth of an image.

On the lower-left edge of the document window is the status bar. The status bar displays the current zoom percentage and information about the image file. Clicking the status bar directly produces a thumbnail showing how the image will print on the paper that is selected in the Page Setup dialog box. Click the arrow at the right end of the status bar to open a menu containing commands that let you see the image in Adobe Bridge or choose the information to be displayed in the status bar (**Figure 9c**).

Figure 9c Click the arrow at the right end of the status bar to choose the information that will be displayed.

Document Window Details

It was briefly mentioned that at the top of the document window you'll find some valuable information like color mode, bit depth, and zoom. Yet, did you know that if there are layers in the file, the name of the current layer is visible before the mode and bit depth (Background, RGB/8)? In addition, if a copyright has been added to the document, a © symbol appears before the name. Also, if the document is unsaved a * appears at the end.

#10 Navigating and Viewing the Document

One way to adjust your view of an image is to use the Navigator panel. Choose Window > Navigator, and then click the Zoom In or Zoom Out buttons or drag the Zoom slider to change your zoom percentage. You can also drag the red rectangular box in the image thumbnail to reposition the portion of the image that is visible in the document window (**Figure 10a**).

Zoom out button
Zoom slider
Zoom in button

Figure 10a Use the Navigator panel to adjust zoom or to realign the image in the document window.

Another way you can zoom and navigate around the image is by using the Zoom and Hand tools (**Figure 10b**). Choose the Zoom tool by clicking its icon in the Tools panel or by pressing the Z key. Next, click on the image to zoom in. Press Alt (Windows) Option (Mac) and click to zoom out. To navigate around the image, choose the Hand tool by clicking its icon in the Tools panel or by pressing the H key. With the Hand tool selected, click and drag to move the image.

— Hand tool

— Zoom tool

Figure 10b The Zoom and Hand tools are the most commonly used navigational tools.

Zoom Shortcuts

Because zooming in and out is something that you will do quite often, it's worthwhile to learn these zoom shortcuts. To zoom in press Ctrl (Windows) Command (Mac) + =. To zoom out press Ctrl (Windows) Command (Mac) + -.

Zoom Fluidity and Flick Panning

New to CS4 is the ability to zoom in/out and to pan with fluidity. Select the Zoom tool and click and hold for fluid zoom. Once you are zoomed in, select the Hand tool and click, drag, and flick the image in one direction. In this way you can "toss" the image with acceleration and friction. Use this technique to quickly move to a new area of your image.

On the other hand, if you are looking for a quicker way to navigate around your image, try this shortcut: While you are zoomed in on the image, press and hold the H key to select the Hand tool. While the H key is pressed, click. This will zoom the image out to a "bird's-eye view" so that you see a navigator-like rectangular box over the image (**Figure 10c**). Drag the box and let go to zoom into that area. This new feature is incredibly fast.

Figure 10c Instead of using the Navigator panel, access the same type of view and functionality by using a shortcut.

When viewing your image, the document window is by default locked into a vertical or horizontal orientation. For even more flexible viewing, you can rotate the canvas by selecting the Rotate Canvas tool (**Figure 10d**) or by pressing and holding the R key. Then click and drag. A compass will appear, and you will be able to freely rotate the document (**Figure 10e**). Keep in mind that this will not affect the pixels. Rather, it is simply a helpful way to view the document while making edits or enhancements. Press the Esc key to exit the Rotate Canvas tool and return the rotation to the default orientation.

Figure 10d The Rotate Canvas tool can be used to freely rotate the document window.

Figure 10e When using the Rotate Canvas tool, a gray and red compass appears superimposed on top of the image. The red needle points to the top of the original orientation.

Note
The features mentioned in #10 are dependent on Open GL and being in an Open GL document. If your computer system's video card doesn't support Open GL or if you are working outside an Open GL window, these features will not be available. If your computer doesn't support Open GL, it's not the end of the world, but it may be time for an upgrade!

#11 Using Full Screen Mode

The Photoshop interface is a rich and powerful work environment, but sometimes its many tools and panels can distract from the image you're working on. You'll find that sometimes it's helpful to strip away some of Photoshop's bells and whistles so that you can concentrate on the image. To this end, Photoshop allows you to choose among three different *screen modes,* which simplify the overall interface to a greater or lesser extent. Choose one of the following modes from the Screen Mode menu (**Figure 11a**):

- **Standard.** The default interface with menu bar in which the image is displayed in a standard document window with a title bar at the top and scroll bars along the side and bottom.

- **Full Screen Mode With Menu Bar.** An interface in which the document window (without title bar or scroll bars) fills the entire screen (except for the menu bar) and is surrounded by light gray.

- **Full Screen Mode.** An interface in which the document window (free of title bar and scroll bars) fills the entire screen (surrounded by a black background), and the menu bar is absent.

Figure 11a Choose a screen mode from the menu in the Application bar.

Simplifying the Interface Quickly

The Full Screen Modes provide a stripped-down environment for editing images. There are times when photographers need to simplify the interface even further so that they can focus on the image. To accomplish this, press Tab to hide the Toolbox and the other panels. Then examine your work in this context, because it may help you discover the weaknesses and the strengths of the image that you might have otherwise overlooked.

Screen Mode Speed Tip

The three different screen modes were designed to help you minimize the interface to focus more on your image. It is the equivalent of cleaning off your desk to focus on the task at hand. Thus, it is a good idea to know how to access these modes quickly. Press the F key to move forward through the different modes. Press Shift + F to move backward.

For photographic work, the ideal mode is Full Screen Mode With Menu Bar. When viewing your images in any screen mode other than Standard, you have the option of changing the background color. Right-click (Windows) Control-click (Mac) on the background and choose Gray, Black, or a Custom color from the context menu (**Figure 11b**).

Figure 11b Use this context menu to change the color of the background when using a nonstandard screen mode.

Tip

If you have chosen one of the two Full Screen Modes, it is best to position the image near the top of the monitor. Select the Hand tool from the Toolbox or press the spacebar to access the Hand tool, and then move the image by dragging. Positioning the image near the top of the monitor will help you have better posture while working in Photoshop.

#12 Understanding Digital Images

Because digital cameras are very much a part of our lives today, it's worth taking a few minutes to delve into the creation of digital images.

When a digital camera snaps a photo, light from the scene being photographed falls onto millions of microscopic electronic sensors. Equally tiny filters separate the light into its red, green, and blue components, just as the cells in the retina of the human eye do; each sensor records the intensity of each of the three colors at that particular location. All this information is converted into numbers and is saved as a digital image file.

As you can probably imagine, the more data points (or *pixels,* for "picture elements") there are in the file, the more accurately the digital image will reproduce the original scene. Because every camera snags pixels in the millions, a camera's data-capturing ability is measured in *megapixels.* Also, the more megapixels an image contains, the more you can enlarge it for printing without losing clarity.

When editing an image in Photoshop, you often adjust its *tonality,* or distribution of light and dark areas. Photoshop has several tools to help you do this, and many of them include a histogram to give you an overview of the tonality of an image. A *histogram* is a simple bar chart that shows how many pixels an image contains at each brightness level. The Levels dialog box contains a histogram with brightness levels starting at 0 (pure black) at the left and increasing to 255 (pure white) at the right (**Figure 12a**).

Figure 12a The histogram in the Levels dialog box. Notice the black-to-white gradient in the Output Levels area—it graphically illustrates the range of brightness levels represented by the histogram.

Understanding how to read a histogram is incredibly helpful for analyzing images. Keep in mind, however, that Photoshop is about more than analysis and description—it is designed to help you to improve your images, too. In Chapter 9, "Modifying Color and Tone," I'll show you how to use the sliders under the shadows, midtones, and highlights regions of the histogram in the Levels dialog box to make adjustments to the range of tonal values in an image.

You don't have to keep a particular dialog box open to track the brightness values in an image. Choose Window > Histogram to open the Histogram panel, which contains nothing but a histogram (**Figure 12b**)! Keep it open while you work to monitor the changes to the distribution of tonalities in your picture.

Figure 12b The Histogram panel (I've added a grayscale ramp of brightness values from 0 to 255 below the panel as a reference). Compare this to the histogram in **Figure 12a**; that image has a pretty good distribution of brightness values, but the tall peak at the left end of the graph shows that this image is very dark.

#13 Resizing Images

Almost every file that is opened in Photoshop will need to be resized. How you resize is important—if something goes wrong, the rest of your Photoshop work will be in vain. Not to worry, you'll master the process of accurate resizing in no time.

When a digital file is created with a digital camera or scanner, a specific amount of information is captured. (Or when you create a new file in Photoshop, you select a specific size containing a specific number of pixels). Once that amount of information is set, you must decide what changes need to be made before the image can be printed, published to the Web, and so on.

Use the Image Size dialog box to resize images. It contains settings for the Pixel Dimensions, Document Size, and Resample Image options, to name a few (**Figure 13a**).

Figure 13a Use the Image Size dialog box to resize images.

The information in the Pixel Dimensions area shows you the amount of information currently in the image. The fields in the Document Size area allow you to set how those pixels will be distributed when you make a print of a certain size. The Resample Image options at the bottom of the window instruct Photoshop on what to do if it has to discard pixels (when sizing down) or create pixels (when sizing up). Here's how the resizing process works:

1. Choose Image > Image size to open the Image Size dialog box.

2. Select the Constrain Proportions check box to maintain the current ratio of pixel width to pixel height.

3. Deselect the Resample Image check box. You don't want to throw away pixels just yet.

4. In the Document Size area, change the resolution to your desired output (for example, 300 pixels/inch).

5. Now select the Resample Image check box.

6. Resize the image. The easiest way to do this is by changing the Height and Width fields in the Document size area to your desired output (for example, 8 × 10 inches).

7. In the Resample Image menu, choose the type of resampling that is recommended in the parentheses next to the interpolation name for the task at hand, and then click OK **(Figure 13b)**.

Nearest Neighbor (preserve hard edges)
Bilinear
Bicubic (best for smooth gradients)
Bicubic Smoother (best for enlargement)
✓ Bicubic Sharper (best for reduction)

Figure 13b Choose the resampling method that is appropriate to the task at hand.

Note
If the proportions of your desired output size are different from those of your image, you won't be able to use the Image Size dialog box to resize your image. In this case, use the method in the following how-to.

#14 Cropping and Straightening Your Images

It is usually best to crop and compose on camera, but there are times when cropping within Photoshop is essential for image resizing or for other creative reasons.

In addition to the resizing method described in the previous how-to, you can also use the Crop tool to resize your images.

To use the Crop tool, select it from the Toolbox or press the shortcut key C, and then enter the desired dimensions and resolution in the options bar. For example, enter 8 in (for inches) in the Width field, 10 in in the Height field, and 300 pixels/inch in the Resolution field (**Figure 14a**).

Figure 14a The options bar when the Crop tool is active.

Next, drag on the image with the Crop tool to draw a marquee around the area you want to keep. You can drag the marquee to reposition it, or drag the marquee handles to resize it. To apply the crop, press Enter (Windows) Return (Mac), double-click inside the marquee, or click the Commit Current Crop Operation button (labeled with a check mark) in the options bar. To cancel the Crop, either press the Cancel button located in the options bar or press the Esc key.

Straightening using the Ruler tool

Have you ever shot a photograph only to notice later that it was crooked? Here is an easy fix for crooked images:

1. Select the Ruler tool (**Figure 14b**).

Figure 14b By default, the Ruler is hidden under the Eyedropper tool. Click and hold on the Eyedropper to access the Ruler. Note that the Eyedropper has been moved up to a higher position in CS4.

2. Find an element(s) in the image that should be horizontal—a line of stonework on a building, for example—and drag the Ruler along that element. In **Figure 14c**, I dragged from the top of one spire to the other.

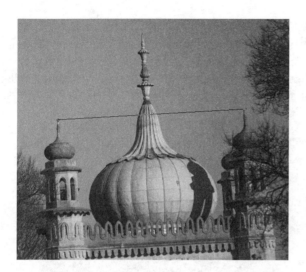

Figure 14c Drag the Ruler tool along a line in your image that *should* be horizontal.

3. To open the Rotate Canvas dialog box, choose Image > Rotate Canvas > Arbitrary (**Figure 14d**).

Figure 14d After drawing a line with the Ruler tool, choose Image > Rotate Canvas > Arbitrary.

4. Click OK to rotate the image. The line you drew with the Ruler tool is now perfectly horizontal.

Composing using the Crop tool

In certain scenarios, it may be helpful to rotate an image when you want to make the composition more dynamic. Take for example this great photograph captured by my wife, Kelly (**Figure 14e**). The rotation in the image makes it dynamic and interesting.

Figure 14e To apply a more standard rotation, choose Image > Rotate Canvas.

To recompose an image using the Crop tool:

1. Select the Crop tool, and then drag within the image to define the crop area.

2. Move your cursor toward one of the four corner points. As the cursor nears a corner point, it changes into a "bent" cursor pointing in two directions, signifying rotation. Click and drag the bent cursor to rotate.

3. Press Enter (Windows) Return (Mac) to apply the crop and view the results. If it doesn't look good on the first try (it often doesn't), don't be dismayed. Press Ctrl + Z (Windows) Command + Z (Mac) to undo and try again.

Note
To apply a more standard rotation, choose Image > Rotate Canvas and choose one of the preset rotation options.

#**15** Saving Images

A crucial step in a Photoshop workflow is to save the image and to save it frequently as you work. The most straightforward way of doing this is to choose File > Save or press Ctrl + S (Windows) Command + S (Mac). If you've already saved the file, you won't see anything—your file will be saved to disk, and you'll be free to continue working.

If this is the first time you've saved the image, the Save As dialog box appears (**Figure 15a**).

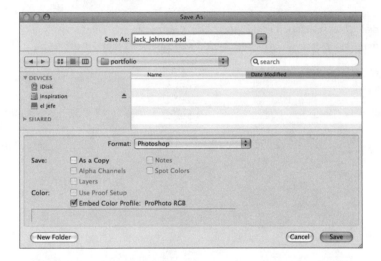

Figure 15a The Save As dialog box.

The Save As dialog box allows you to define several file parameters, chief among them the file's name and its format. In fact, if you ever want to change the name or format of a file that's already been saved, choose File > Save As or type Ctrl + Shift + S (Windows) Command + Shift + S (Mac) to summon the Save As dialog box. If your image file includes layers and you want to preserve those layers in the new file, remember that you need to save your document in PSD, PSB (Large Document), PDF (Photoshop PDF), or TIFF format.

Another important step when saving files is to select the Embed Color Profile check box. This will "tag" your document with a specific color profile. By way of analogy, you can think of color profiles as similar to size tags on clothing (in essence, Small, Medium, Large). The size tags clarify the garment's dimensions and take the guesswork out of shopping. In the same way, Embed Color Profile takes the guesswork out of color and leads to more accurate color reproduction.

Changing the Format of Multiple Images Quickly

You can change the format of multiple images quickly using Photoshop's Image Processor script rather than opening multiple images and saving them one at a time. Choose File > Scripts > Image Processor. In the Image Processor dialog box, select a folder of images to be converted to a specific file type and/or resized to dimensions of your choosing, and then click Run (**Figure 15b**).

Figure 15b Use the Image Processor script to convert and process multiple files at one time.

CHAPTER THREE

Using Adobe Bridge

Ansel Adams grew up in Marin, California, just across the bay from San Francisco before the Golden Gate Bridge was built. As an adult, the bridge played an important role in Ansel's photographic journey, because it gave him newfound, easy access to not only the great and scenic city of San Francisco, but also to the absolute architectural and scenic beauty of the Golden Gate.

In many ways, you can think of Adobe Bridge as not unlike Ansel Adams' Golden Gate: It provides unique access to your images and for many photographers has become an integral and enjoyable part of their creative workflow.

Adobe Bridge is an access-point application designed to help you browse, locate, and organize your images. It also can help you import, edit, process, and even order prints without ever launching Photoshop. While you may find you often use Bridge instead of Photoshop, keep in mind that the two applications make great teammates. One of the main reasons that Bridge is gaining prominence is because it allows you to open images directly into the Adobe Camera Raw plug-in, where you have access to a wealth of sophisticated image-editing tools. And Adobe Camera Raw isn't just for raw images—you can also use it with images in the JPEG and TIFF formats.

#16 Modifying Bridge Preferences

If you are going to make the leap to using Bridge, you'll want to get your preferences dialed in. Choose Edit > Preferences (Windows) or Bridge > Preferences (Mac) to launch the Preferences dialog box (**Figure 16a**).

Figure 16a The Bridge Preferences dialog box showing the General pane.

Tip
The keyboard shortcut for opening the Preferences dialog box is the same in Bridge as in Photoshop: Ctrl + K (Windows) Command + K (Mac).

Most of the default preference settings are fine, so let's focus only on those that are most important to modify.

In the Appearance area of the General pane, verify that the settings for User Interface Brightness and Image Backdrop are what you want. Drag the Image Backdrop slider to the left or right to change the brightness of the Content and Preview panels. Drag the User Interface Brightness slider to change the brightness of the Favorites, Folders, Filter, and Metadata panels, as well as the borders of the interface. Keep in mind that the

Image Backdrop color will also be designated as the background color for slide shows, Review mode, or Full Screen mode (learn more about Review mode in how-to #21 and about slide shows in how-to #23). Next, click the option Ctrl (Windows) Command (Mac) + Click Opens the Loupe When Previewing or Reviewing. By adding the extra shortcut key you won't accidentally open the Loupe when you click on the image.

Bridge allows you to assign colored labels to your images, which are very handy for organizing your files. Although the colors are hardwired into Bridge, you can choose your own names for the labels. Switch to the Labels pane, where you can enter custom text for each label (**Figure 16b**).

No Pane, No Gain

The Preferences dialog box in Bridge is organized just like its equivalent in Photoshop. If you need a quick refresher course in navigating the dialog box's options, see how-to #2, Modifying Preferences.

Figure 16b In the Labels preferences, you can apply custom names to labels.

I like to use a red label for my best images, so I've changed the name of the red label to "yahhhooo!" Make sure the option Require the Command Key to Apply Labels and Ratings is deselected. This will speed up your image rating and organizing workflow.

Last but not least are the options in the Cache preference pane. *Cache* refers to the area on your hard disk that Bridge uses to store descriptive information (including thumbnails) about the files that you view in Bridge. By default, Bridge uses a centralized cache, which works well when your files are always stored on one drive and on one computer. However, if

Labels in Photoshop and Lightroom

Lightroom is becoming more and more popular with photographers. If you use Adobe Bridge and Adobe Photoshop Lightroom, be sure to use the same custom names for your labels in Bridge that you use for your labels in Lightroom. That way both programs will be able to recognize the same set of labels.

Photoshop Bridge Shortcut

The more you use Bridge, the more frequently you will navigate back and forth between Photoshop and Bridge. The shortcut for navigating between Photoshop and Bridge is Ctrl + Alt + O (Windows) Command + Option + O (Mac). You can use this shortcut from either application. In Photoshop, use the shortcut to open Bridge. In Bridge, use the shortcut to open Photoshop.

you're like me and your images travel around quite a bit, you'll want to select the option Automatically Export Cache To Folders When Possible (**Figure 16c**). This will give you the most flexibility and is the best option if you use multiple hard drives or if the images will be accessed on multiple computers.

Figure 16c In the Cache Preferences pane, select Automatically Export Cache To Folders When Possible for the most flexibility.

#17 Working with the Bridge Interface

You can configure Bridge to fit your workflow needs. You may at times want to use Bridge as if it were a big, functional tool like a sledgehammer—hammering through the organizing and processing of a large number of images. Other times you may want to use it as if it were a small detail tool like a wood carver's chisel—slowly and artistically chipping away at organizing and processing a small group of your best images.

At the top of the Bridge window you will find tools for navigating through folders, creating new folders, rotating or deleting images, and more. The main Bridge interface is made up of various panels (**Figure 17a**).

Content panel
Folders panel
Path bar
Favorites panel
Collection panel
Filter panel
Workspace buttons
Preview panel
Metadata panel
Image thumbnail
Keywords panel

Figure 17a The default workspace in Bridge.

At the heart of the interface is the Content panel, which displays thumbnails of the images contained in the active folder. Accompanying the Content panel are a number of other panels, which may be visible or hidden, depending on how you've configured your workspace:

- **Folders** allows you to navigate the folder hierarchy on your hard drive.

- **Favorites** offers you quick access to frequently used folders.

- **Filter** allows you to display a limited selection of files based on criteria you choose.

(continued on next page)

- **Collections** allows you to create folder-independent groups of images based on different criteria.

- **Content** displays the thumbnail previews.

- **Metadata** displays the metadata for the selected file (or files).

- **Keywords** lets you assign keywords to images.

- **Preview** displays a larger view of the selected image.

(There's also an Inspector panel, but it is used only with Version Cue and is a feature that is beyond the scope of this book).

You can arrange the panels to create a workspace that suits your working style. Move a panel by dragging its tab or resize panels by dragging the horizontal or vertical divider bar that separates them. Once you have the panels arranged the way you like them, you can save the arrangement as a custom workspace by choosing Window > Workspace > New Workspace and giving it a distinctive name. Your custom workspace will then appear on the Workspace submenu (Window > Workspace) along with the other preconfigured workspaces that ship with Bridge.

To select either a preconfigured workspace or a custom workspace, click one of the workspace buttons (**Figure 17b**) or press the appropriate shortcut key. In addition, you can change the workspace button order and the shortcut key. To change the order, click and drag a tab to a new location (**Figure 17c**). The tab in position one will always have the shortcut Ctrl (Windows) Command (Mac) + F1, position two Ctrl (Windows) Command (Mac) + F2, and so on.

	ESSENTIALS	FILMSTRIP	METADATA	OUTPUT	KEYWORDS	PREVIEW	LIGHT TABLE
Command (Mac) + Ctrl (Windows)	F1	F2	F3	F4	F5	F6	F7

Figure 17b Quickly change the Bridge workspace by clicking one of the preconfigured workspace buttons.

	ESSENTIALS	FILMSTRIP	METADATA	OUTPUT	KEYWORDS	PREVIEW	LIGHT TABLE	Original
	ESSENTIALS	OUTPUT	KEYWORDS	PREVIEW	LIGHT TABLE	FILMSTRIP	METADATA	Customer order
Command (Mac) + Ctrl (Windows)	F1	F2	F3	F4	F5	F6	F7	

Figure 17c The top graphic shows the original workspace button positions. Below, the workspaces have been modified, but the shortcuts stay the same.

In addition, at the top of the Bridge interface there are some more detailed controls worth noting. On the top left you'll find icons that allow you to view recent files/folders, get photos, review and refine your images, open Camera Raw, and open the Output (PDF/Web) workspace (**Figure 17d**). On the top right you'll find icons that allow you to view different image previews, sort, rotate, view recent files/folders, create a new folder, and delete.

Figure 17d Use these icons to access some of the more frequently needed controls and tools within Bridge.

Bridge Speed Tips

- The quickest way to expand or collapse a specific panel is to double-click the panel's tab. You can also double-click either vertical divider bar to collapse the panels on that side of the Content panel.

- Choose a different workspace from each of the numbered menus in the lower-right corner of the window. Then simply click a number to switch to the workspace you've chosen from that menu.

- Right-click (Windows) Control-click (Mac) any thumbnail(s) to open a context menu that contains many commands, including Open, Copy, Reveal in Finder, Batch Rename, Label, and more.

#18 Rating, Sorting, and Searching

Whether you're capturing an event with a digital camera or creating Web site design variations for a client, it seems that today you're creating more content than ever before. The upside of all this content creation is that it makes for an incredibly exciting time full of unprecedented discovery and creativity. The downside is that most of your thousands of digital files are completely unorganized and, as a result, seemingly inaccessible. Of course, this is one of the main functions of Bridge—to help you keep all your creative efforts within easy reach. Here's a good way to use Bridge to that effect:

Note
When you are ready to review and edit your images, plan on making multiple editing passes—in essence, be sure to go through your images more than once.

1. Click the first image of the set to display it in the Preview panel.

2. Press the arrow key to select and preview the next image.

3. Continue previewing your images and, as you do this, assign labels, star ratings, or a combination of both to the files. To do this, choose the appropriate label or rating from the Label menu. When an image has a label applied, it shows up as a strip of color beneath its thumbnail in the Content panel. Ratings appear as a row of stars within the colored label (**Figure 18a**).

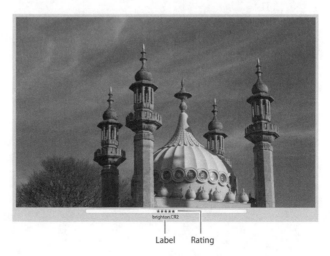

brighton.CR2

Label   Rating

Figure 18a Once you've selected a label and/or a rating for an image, they will be appended to the image thumbnail.

It's a good idea to employ a specific strategy for your rating system. For example, on my first passes, I tend to rate the keeper images as four or five stars by holding Ctrl (Windows) Command (Mac) and pressing 4 (or 5). Then in the Filter panel, I click the criteria that correspond to the images I want to see (**Figure 18b**).

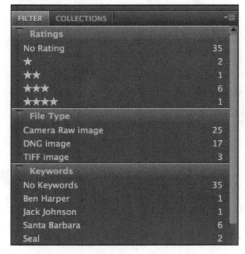

Figure 18b Choose criteria in the Filter panel to filter and display images that meet those criteria.

Bridge Overview

To get up to speed on how best to use Bridge, you can find a free Bridge video tutorial at http://tv.adobe.com.

Filtering Shortcut

Here is a valuable shortcut you won't find anywhere else! If you want to filter your images so you see only those with a specific rating or label, hold Ctrl + Alt (Windows) Command + Option (Mac) and press any key from 1 through 9. This is a quicker alternative to clicking an item in the Ratings or Labels categories in the Filter panel.

If you need to find a file by more specific parameters, such as by the date it was created or its dimensions, select Edit > Find or press Ctrl + F (Windows) Command + F (Mac). This will launch the Find dialog box, where you can add specific details for your search. Choose an item from the first menu in the Criteria area to search by Filename, Date Created, File Size, Height, Width, Keyword, Label, ISO, and more (**Figure 18c**).

Figure 18c The Find dialog box offers many options for image searching.

#19 Working with Collections

Collections are another much needed new feature in Bridge CS4 because they give you the ability to group photos in a way that isn't dependent on the folder they are located in. In other words, you can create a group of photos even if they are not located in the same folder.

The Collections panel (**Figure 19a**) allows you to create, locate, open, and edit your collections. There are two main types of collections: Collections and Smart Collections. Collections are groups that you make by simply choosing and adding photos. Smart Collections, on the other hand, are typically based on the results of searching for images with particular criteria (e.g., photos with a four star rating or photos captured by a particular camera, etc.).

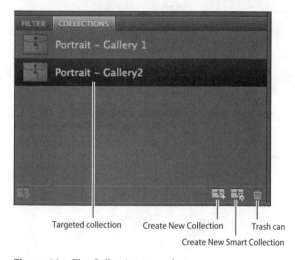

Targeted collection   Create New Collection   Trash can
Create New Smart Collection

Figure 19a The Collections panel.

You can create a new Collection with or without images. To create a new and empty collection, click the New Collection button at the bottom of the Collections panel to create a new, empty collection. Or to create a collection with images, first select one or more photos in the Bridge Content panel. Next, click the New Collection button in the Collections panel. A dialog box appears; click Yes to include the selected files in the new collection.

Now that you have created the collection, adding or removing files is a breeze. To add files, simply drag them from the Content panel to the

54

collection name. To remove files from a collection, select the file in the Content panel and click Remove From Collection (**Figure 19b**).

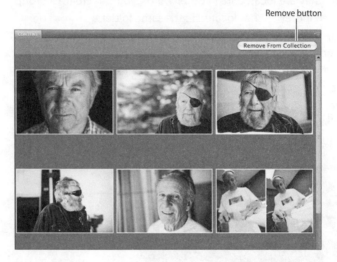

Remove button

Figure 19b Click the Remove button or right-click (Windows) Control-click (Mac) to remove files from a collection using the context menu.

Tip
To delete a collection, navigate to the Collections panel, click on the collection name, and drag it to the trash icon.

Tip
Renaming any type of collection is actually quite easy. Simply double-click the collection name and type a new name. Or right-click (Windows) Control-click (Mac) the collection and choose Rename. Type in a new name.

Working with Smart Collections is a bit different than regular Collections. Smart Collections are built based on search criteria, so you can take advantage of descriptive metadata and build a collection based on specifics that you have defined. To create a Smart Collection, click the Create New Smart Collection button (Figure 19a) at the bottom of the Collections panel. The Smart Collection dialog box opens (**Figure 19c**). Use this dialog to determine the criteria for the Smart Collection. Choose a particular folder. Next, choose the criteria out of over 20 different options—for example, Focal Length and Color Mode. Then refine the result to determine which images will be included. Click OK.

Define Source folder ——
Click to add/delete criteria
Refine collection results criteria ——

Figure 19c The Smart Collection dialog box.

Note
When creating a Smart Collection for All Subfolders and for Non-indexed Files, be prepared to wait for a bit because it will take Photoshop some time to go through all the images and build the Smart Collection.

#20 Modifying Metadata and Keywords

Many of the powerful Bridge features that allow you to organize, search, and keep track of your files and versions depend on the metadata in your files. Essentially, metadata is a set of standardized information about a file, such as the author name, copyright, keywords, the camera settings in force when the image was created, and so on. In other words, metadata is data about data. You can consider an image to be nothing more than data, and the metadata is the information that describes the image, such as the file type, the size, or the date it was captured.

In sum, metadata is valuable because you can use it to streamline your workflow and organize your files. Bridge provides two ways of working with metadata: through the Metadata panel and through the File Info dialog box.

Let's begin with the File Info dialog box. Select an image, and then choose File > File Info (**Figure 20a**).

Figure 20a Use the File Info dialog box to view or edit an image's metadata.

This dialog box displays quite a bit of information. At first glance, it may look a little like overkill, but many of the settings in it are important. In particular, you may want to add keywords and copyright information.

Editing metadata within Bridge is easier than ever. For example, choose Window > Workspace > Keywords to edit metadata keywords. Notice the Keywords and Filter panels on the left. Adding keywords to your images is a critical step in digital asset management, so let's begin there:

1. Working in the Keywords panel, click the New Keyword button or New Sub Keyword button (or choose either New Keyword or New Sub Keyword from the panel menu). A new default name appears in the panel.

2. To create the new keyword or new sub keyword, type over the default name and press Enter (Windows) Return (Mac) (**Figure 20b**).

Figure 20b Use the Keywords panel to create keywords or to assign keywords to images.

Select the Metadata workspace to view and edit more general metadata. The top of the panel is occupied by the metadata placard, which displays the settings from the camera when the picture was taken. You'll find information such as the aperture setting, shutter speed, metering mode, ISO, file size, pixel dimensions, and color space. The placard is formatted

Adding Keywords Training Video

Be sure to check out the free Adobe training video on adding keywords at http://tv.adobe.com

to resemble the LCD screen on a camera, so you most likely will find it a very useful feature of Bridge (**Figure 20c**).

Metadata placard —

Figure 20c The metadata placard contains an easy-to-understand visualization of valuable information.

Perhaps the most important part of the Metadata panel is the IPTC Core. This is where you can add or modify keywords, copyright, contact information, and more. Click the triangle to the left of the IPTC Core heading to expand the IPTC Core section, select an item, and start typing.

#21 Using Review Mode

As the name implies, Review mode is a new CS4 view mode that is helpful for evaluating your images. It provides you with a full-screen preview of selected files in a carousel-like view. And of course there is more: Not only can you view your image, but you can also rotate and rate images, remove images from the selection, and save selected files as a collection. To use the Review mode, follow these steps:

1. In Adobe Bridge, select a folder of images or select the images you want to review.

2. Choose View > Review Mode or press Ctrl + B (Windows) Command (Mac) + B to enter Review mode. You will see your images in a carousel-like layout (**Figure 21a**).

Figure 21a Review mode allows you to view a set of images in full-screen mode. This is especially helpful when you are evaluating which images in a set are best.

3. Before you begin to work in Review mode, press H to reveal the keyboard shortcuts (**Figure 21b**) for working in Review mode. Press H again to hide the shortcuts.

(continued on next page)

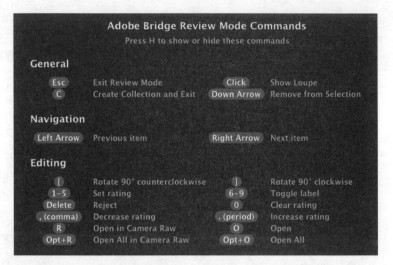

Figure 21b The Review mode shortcut keys.

4. To begin working in Review mode, do any of the following:

- Use the controls (**Figure 21c**) at the bottom of the view mode to navigate to the other images, remove images from the selection, access the Loupe tool, add image(s) to a collection, or to exit.

Preview image
Next image
Remove from selection

Loope tool
Add to collection
Exit button

Figure 21c The controls at the bottom of Review mode.

- Click the Left Arrow or Right Arrow keys on your keyboard to navigate to the previous or next images.

- Click the Down Arrow key to remove image(s) from the selection.

- Click on any image in the background to view it in the front as the largest image.

- Right-click (Windows) Control-click (Mac) any image to rate it, apply a label, rotate it, or open it.

- Press one of the bracket keys to rotate the image. Press] to rotate the foreground image 90° clockwise. Press [to rotate the image 90° counterclockwise.

Tip
The quickest way to exit Review mode is to press the Esc key.

Note
To learn more about Review mode, be sure to watch the video tutorial on Previewing and comparing images at: http://tv.adobe.com.

#22 Using the Loupe Tool

For those times when you need to examine an image closely, the Loupe tool comes in handy. By default, the Loupe tool magnifies a portion of your image to 100 percent (that is, to the level of individual pixels), but you can change the magnification.

To use the Loupe tool:

1. Select an image thumbnail in the Content panel.

2. Click the image in the Preview panel. A virtual loupe appears on the screen displaying an enlarged view of the portion of the image where you clicked (**Figure 22a**).

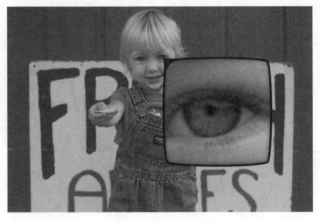

Figure 22a Use the Loupe tool to zoom in on an image preview to check for focus and detail.

3. Drag the Loupe tool to view different areas of the image.

4. If you want a closer look, press the equals key (=). To zoom out, press the minus key (−).

5. To dismiss the Loupe tool, single-click inside the magnified area or click the X in the bottom right of the Loupe.

One of the ways the Loupe tool is most helpful is in examining several images at once. For example, you can use it to compare the sharpness of multiple similar images:

1. In Bridge, Ctrl-click (Windows) Command-click (Mac) the images you want to compare. The images will appear in the Preview panel.

2. In the Preview panel, click the first of the images you want to compare to open the Loupe tool.

3. Click the second image you want to compare to open another Loupe tool. Continue clicking image previews until you have as many Loupe tools open as you need (**Figure 22b**).

Figure 22b Use the Loupe tool to compare similar images. In this case, both previews look sharp; however, the Loupe tool reveals that the lower image is a higher-quality image.

Zoom and Reposition Multiple Loupes

When you have multiple Loupe tools open at the same time, press Ctrl (Windows) Command (Mac) with the plus key (+) or minus key (−) to zoom all Loupes in and out simultaneously.

To reposition multiple Loupe tools at the same time, hold down Ctrl (Windows) Command (Mac) and drag one of the Loupe tools. All active Loupes will move simultaneously.

Tip
You can access and use the Loupe tool in Review mode (#21). All the short-cuts are identical to using the Loupe in Bridge.

Note
By default, the Loupe tool opens when you click on an image in the Pre-view panel or Review mode. For even better control, choose Bridge > Preferences and select Ctrl (Windows) Command (Mac) + Click Opens the Loupe When Previewing or Reviewing. This way you won't inadver-tently open the Loupe because it will only open when you click with the additional shortcut key.

#23 Viewing a Slide Show

Fullscreen View

The Slideshow view is undoubtedly a great way to view and show your images. Yet, new to CS4 is the ability to view one or more images in Full Screen view mode. Use this mode when you want to quickly view your work while minimizing the complexity of the Bridge interface. Think of this view as Slideshow's "younger brother"; it is very similar to the Slideshow view but without all the grown up features. Select one or more images, choose View > Fullscreen or press the spacebar. Press the arrow keys to navigate through the selected images.

There is nothing better than clearing away the clutter, dimming the lights, and watching a slide show of compelling work. Bridge has several features that can make this experience a reality.

Choose View > Slideshow or press Ctrl + L (Windows) Command + L (Mac) to launch a slide show of the images in the current folder. Then in Slideshow view press the H key to display a list of commands for working with the slide show (**Figure 23a**).

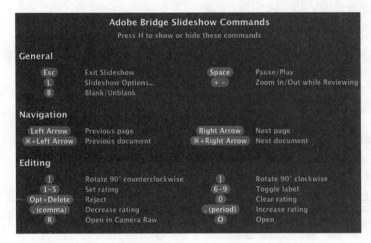

Figure 23a While in Slideshow view, press H to display commands for slide shows.

To customize the slide show, while in Slideshow view, press the L key. The Slideshow Options dialog box appears. Here you can modify options for the overall display and for individual slides (**Figure 23b**).

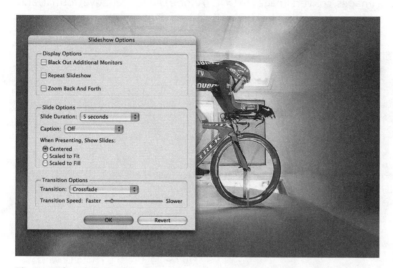

Figure 23b While in Slideshow view, press L to open the Slideshow Options dialog box.

#24 Using the Photo Downloader

The Photo Downloader is an excellent tool that gives you the ability to import photos from your digital camera or other digital media device. The application lets you specify a location for the downloaded files, rename the images, convert images to DNG (Adobe Digital Negative) format, and save copies to another hard drive if desired (**Figure 24**).

Figure 24 Use the Photo Downloader to download photos from your digital camera or digital media storage device.

To use the Photo Downloader:

1. Connect your camera or card reader to the computer.

2. Choose File > Get Photos From Camera.

3. Select the name of the camera or card reader from the Get Photos From menu. Most likely, the currently attached camera or device will be selected by default.

4. Choose the folder location. Ideally, create a folder structure that is consistent and easy to understand.

5. To rename the files as you import them, choose an option from the Rename Files menu. If you are renaming your images, be sure to use a naming convention that is consistent so that one or two years from now you'll be able to easily access and find the images you need.

6. If you prefer to have Bridge open once the import is complete, select Open Adobe Bridge. This allows you to focus on other tasks while the images are being imported. When the import is complete, Bridge opens, directing your attention to the images.

7. If you are shooting in your camera's raw format, you may want to consider selecting the Convert to DNG option so that your images will be converted to the DNG format upon import. (For more on DNG, see Chapter 4, "Using Adobe Camera Raw.")

8. New to the CS4 dialog box is the ability to Delete Originals. Use this option if you would like to permanently delete the files from the media storage device (e.g., a Compact Flash memory card).

9. To save copies of photos as you import them, select Save Copies To and specify a location. Of course, one of the most important steps in managing your digital assets is to back them up. A great way to get a jumpstart on backup is to save copies of your images to a separate hard drive.

Apply Metadata on Import

If you want to apply metadata to your images as they are imported, click the Advanced Dialog button and type information in the Author and Copyright text boxes, or choose a metadata template from the Template menu. This lets you add your copyright to your images while they're being imported. Now that's what I call optimizing your photographic workflow!

#25 Using the "Power Tools" in Bridge

Bridge is equipped with some heavy-duty power tools, which you'll find on the Photoshop submenu (Tools > Photoshop) (**Figure 25**).

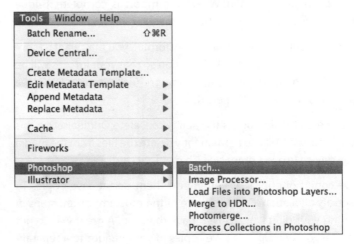

Figure 25 The Photoshop submenu gives you a direct link to some powerful commands within Photoshop.

You'll find identical commands on the Automate submenu (File > Automate) in Photoshop, and in fact, using any of these commands from Bridge will fire up Photoshop, where the operations will actually be carried out. A few of these are covered later in the book, but briefly reviewing them here will help you become aware of their basic functions.

Batch

The Batch command applies a Photoshop action (a saved series of commands) to multiple files. Using the Batch command, you can automate and speed up your workflow by leaps and bounds.

Image processor

The image processor provides an effective and efficient way to "batch" resize and convert a small or large number of images. This tool is especially helpful when you need to deliver TIFFs or JPEGs to a client (or anyone else for that matter) at a specific size, color space, and dimension.

Load Files into Photoshop Layers

Brand new to Photoshop CS4 is the Load Files into Photoshop Layers tool. It gives you the ability to select two or more images and to open them into single layered documents in Photoshop. You'll find this especially helpful for creative endeavors like building a multilayered composite or for more technical tasks like combining two exposures of the same subject matter. Whatever your needs, you'll soon discover that this is a tool you will use quite frequently.

Merge to HDR

Merge to HDR (High Dynamic Range) combines multiple exposures of the same subject into a single image. The goal with HDR is to achieve a far greater dynamic range of exposure than would be possible in one single exposure. For example, if you're shooting in an environment with a wide range of lighting conditions, such as dark shadows and bright highlights, you can take several images of the scene using different exposure settings and use Merge to HDR to combine them into one image that captures the full dynamic range of the subject.

Photomerge

The majority of panoramic photographs are created with a tool like Photomerge. You take multiple photographs of a panoramic scene and then "stitch" together the images with Photomerge. If you've never tried creating a panorama, I highly recommend it. The format is cinematic and can't be taken in with a simple glance. Instead, it draws viewers in, because they have to visually travel through the photograph.

Process Collections in Photoshop

The new Process Collections in Photoshop tool is helpful for creating panoramic or HDR photographs. It works by examining your photos to see if they have been taken within 18 seconds of each other, and then it decides if the photos should be an HDR or a panorama and blends them together in Photoshop. That said, this does take quite a bit of processing power and time to put the HDR or panorama together.

Bridge Output Features

If you previously used Bridge CS3, you may be wondering about a few of the other Photoshop tools that appear to be missing. In particular, Contact Sheet, PDF, PDF Presentation, Picture Package, and Web Photogallery. Well there is no need to worry; these tools have not been removed, just relocated. You can access these features by navigating to the Output workspace. For more information see Chapter 14, "Output."

CHAPTER FOUR

Using Photoshop Camera Raw

The Photoshop Camera Raw plug-in allows you to open raw image files from many different types of digital cameras directly into Photoshop. Using this plug-in is becoming a more integral part of one's digital imaging workflow. It is so important in fact that this is actually the longest chapter in the whole book. Camera Raw is flexible and powerful, and it gives you the ability to make nondestructive edits to your images. More than anything, Camera Raw can empower you to accomplish more creative and higher-quality results.

In this chapter, you will learn the essentials of the Photoshop Camera Raw plug-in. You'll learn how to adjust exposure, color, tone, saturation, sharpness, and more. You'll learn professional tips for creating amazing black-and-white images. You will gain skills in retouching raw images, red eye removal, cropping, and noise reduction. In addition, you'll learn how to apply your new skills in a way that will expedite your workflow.

#26 Understanding Photoshop Camera Raw

The Photoshop Camera Raw plug-in provides a unique and compelling way to process raw, JPEG, and TIFF files inside Photoshop. Camera Raw offers a number of different controls to modify exposure, color, tone, contrast, sharpness, and so on. What is unique about Camera Raw is that when you use it to make an adjustment, the data in your image is not changed; rather, the plug-in creates a set of instructions that determine how the pixels in the image are to be displayed.

You can think of a camera raw file as a traditional film negative. If you want to create different types of prints from a film negative, the film negative never actually changes. Rather, you could bring the negative to a photo lab and write down instructions for the lab to print the image brighter, darker, or as a sepia tone. The negative stays the same, but the final output varies based on the written instructions.

In comparison, a raw file (like a negative) is never modified, but the set of adjustment instructions can be infinitely modified. The wonderful thing about this approach is that the image adjustments are not permanent, and they do not drastically increase the file size. Thus, making adjustments with Camera Raw keeps you nimble, creative, and quick.

When you use Camera Raw, the adjustments (or "instructions") you make are stored as metadata. The metadata is saved in one of the following ways:

- As a database (the default storage method)

- As an accompanying sidecar file (an extensible Metadata Platform [XMP] file)

- Within the file (DNG format—a nonproprietary, TIFF-based file format for storing Camera Raw data)

Which option is best? It really depends on your preferences, so let's discuss the options. By default, Camera Raw is set to save the camera raw "instructions" in a database. This option is best if you are working on only one computer, and the image will stay on that computer.

For the majority of amateur and pro imagemakers, this default setting isn't ideal because of the need to store a large volume of images. Multiple hard drives are usually necessary. If this is your situation, you may want to change the default preference to accommodate this need. Open Adobe Bridge and choose Edit > Camera Raw Preferences (Windows) or Bridge > Camera Raw Preferences (Mac) to display the Camera Raw Preferences dialog box (**Figure 26a**). From the Save Image Settings In menu, choose Sidecar ".xmp" Files. This provides more flexibility, since the raw settings will "travel" with the image rather than stay on the main computer's hard drive.

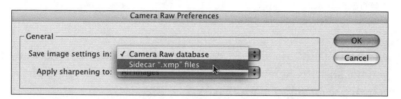

Figure 26a Have Bridge save adjustment changes in sidecar files for more flexibility.

The other option is to convert your images to DNG format, which will store the camera raw settings inside the actual file. You can convert your images to the DNG format using Adobe's DNG Converter application or by saving them from within Camera Raw as DNG files. For more information on the DNG format and DNG Converter, see www.adobe.com/products/dng.

To use Camera Raw with JPEG and/or TIFF files, open the Camera Raw Preferences dialog box in Bridge and select the check box for the appropriate option in the JPEG and TIFF Handling area (**Figure 26b**).

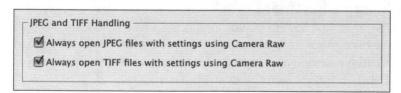

Figure 26b Select one or both of these options to open images in the JPEG or TIFF formats in the Camera Raw plug-in.

Learn More About the DNG Format

If you would like more information regarding the DNG format, visit www.adobe.com/products/dng.

Opening Files in Camera Raw

The best way to open JPEGs, TIFFs, or raw files in Camera Raw is to use Adobe Bridge. In Bridge, select an image, and then choose File > Open In Camera Raw.

To open raw images directly into Camera Raw from within Photoshop, choose File > Open, and then navigate to the raw image file.

#27 Learning the Camera Raw Interface

Open an image in Camera Raw from within Photoshop or Bridge. Notice that the interface looks different than Photoshop or Bridge because the plug-in works like a stand-alone application. To get the most out of Camera Raw, you need to become familiar with the main aspects of its interface.

Tools

At the top of the Camera Raw dialog box is a row of tools. These tools give you the ability perform various important functions—everything from zooming to rotating (**Figure 27a**).

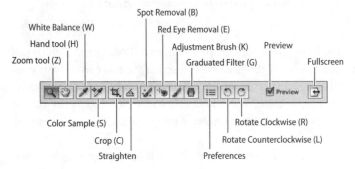

Figure 27a Camera Raw tools and the respective shortcut keys.

Image adjustment tabs

The bulk of the power and functionality of Camera Raw can be found in the controls collected into eight image adjustment tabs. Click a tab to access the controls it contains. Each tab uses a somewhat cryptic icon as a label—here's the secret decoder ring (**Figure 27b**):

Figure 27b The Camera Raw image adjustment tabs and their functions.

- **Basic.** Adjust white balance, exposure, contrast, saturation.

- **Tone Curve.** Fine-tune tonality.

- **Detail.** Adjust sharpening and reduce noise.

- **HSL/Grayscale.** Convert to color or black and white.

- **Split Toning.** Add color to the highlights and shadows.

- **Lens Corrections.** Fix lens vignetting and chromatic aberration.

- **Camera Calibration.** Customize settings for a specific camera.

- **Presets.** Save and access presets.

Save, Open, Cancel, and Done

When you are finished adjusting your image, click one of the four buttons along the bottom of the Camera Raw window (**Figure 27c**):

- **Save Image.** Save the raw file in a different file format (PSD, TIFF, DNG, JPEG).

- **Open Image.** Open the image in Photoshop.

- **Cancel.** Cancel adjustments and return to Bridge.

- **Done.** Apply adjustments and return to Bridge.

Figure 27c When your work in Camera Raw is done, click one of the four buttons.

Tip
While in Camera Raw, press Alt (Windows) Option (Mac) to change some of the button options. For example, Open becomes Open Copy, Cancel becomes Rest, and Save becomes Save Without Viewing the Save Dialog Box.

Devote Your Entire Screen to Camera Raw

When working in Camera Raw, it's a good idea to always work in Full Screen mode. This will help you focus on the image. Click the Toggle Full Screen button or press the F key to go to Full Screen mode. Click the button (or press F) again to go back to windowed mode. Camera Raw remembers your setting, even if you close the window and open it again.

#28 Setting the White Balance

A correct White Balance setting ensures that neutral colors, like grays and white, are actually gray or white rather than tinged with yellow or blue. In addition, by correcting the neutrals, you simultaneously fix any unnatural color shifts that exist in the image.

The Basic tab in the Camera Raw interface has three controls for correcting a color shift in an image: White Balance, Temperature, and Tint. From the White Balance menu, choose a specific lighting environment to fine-tune the color balance (**Figure 28**):

- **As Shot.** Uses the White Balance settings chosen by the camera at the moment the picture was taken.

- **Auto.** Camera Raw calculates a new white balance based on the image data.

- **Daylight, Cloudy, Shade, Tungsten, Fluorescent, or Flash.** Camera Raw calculates a new white balance based on the color temperature of the selected lighting condition.

Figure 28 White Balance options.

To fine-tune the white balance, adjust the Temperature and Tint sliders. Adjusting the Temperature slider makes the image warmer or cooler. Adjusting the Tint slider compensates for a green or magenta tint.

Accessing the White Balance setting through the Basic panel to correct white balance works fine; however, one of the quickest and easiest ways to remove color shift in an image is to use the White Balance tool on the main toolbar in Camera Raw. This tool can be used to specify that an object should be white or gray. By doing this, Camera Raw can determine the color of the light in which the scene was shot, and then adjust for scene lighting automatically.

Select the White Balance tool and click on an object in the image that you know should be a neutral gray or white.

Note
When using the White Balance tool and choosing a white area to click, be sure to choose a white area that contains significant white detail rather than a specular (or shiny) highlight. Sometimes selecting an area that is off-white or gray works best.

Tip
You can double-click the White Balance tool icon to reset the white balance to As Shot.

White Balance and the Human Eye

The human eye is incredibly adaptable. Thus, when you first begin to work on digital images, it's difficult to identify color problems. Consider what happens when you wear sunglasses with a yellow tint. After wearing the glasses for a few moments, you actually stop seeing (or noticing) the yellow color shift, but once you remove the glasses you notice the shift. This is a result of the adaptability of the human eye. Therefore, we need tools like the White Balance tool to help us notice color inconsistencies. Also, an added benefit of using the White Balance tool is that it will train your eye to see color shifts, so you eventually will be able to fix color problems more effectively.

#29 Adjusting Exposure and Tone Automatically

Auto Correction Improvements

If you tried using Auto Correction in a previous version of Photoshop, you may have discovered that the results were not always desirable. But don't let your past experience cause you to overlook this powerful feature. Now in CS4, thanks to new significant Camera Raw improvements, the Auto Correction feature works much better.

As a professional photographer, I spend the majority of my time in Camera Raw adjusting exposure and tone. There are two options for making these adjustments: Use the Auto option or make custom adjustments using various sliders in the section of the Basic tab that contains tone controls. (The latter is discussed in #30.)

Let's first examine the Auto option.

The Auto button is located at the top of the tone controls section (**Figure 29**). When you click the Auto button, Camera Raw analyzes the raw image data in the file and makes automatic adjustments to tone controls, such as Exposure, Recovery, Blacks, Brightness, and Contrast. Three main situations make it advantageous to use the Auto option:

- If you shoot a high volume of images and don't have time to dial in specific tone settings, selecting Auto will greatly speed up your workflow.

- If you want an initial idea of the best settings for your image. Auto doesn't always produce perfect results, but it can give you insight into what adjustments may be needed.

- If you are new to Camera Raw, Auto can be used as a starting point. Click Auto and then fine-tune the image with the adjustment sliders.

Figure 29 Click Auto to apply tone adjustments automatically.

#30 Adjusting Custom Exposure and Tone

If you want to take your images to the next level, use the Exposure and tone sliders located in the Basic tab (**Figure 30a**). The sliders are simple and intuitive.

Figure 30a Adjust exposure and tone as desired using these adjustment sliders.

The descriptions of each control follows:

- **Exposure.** This slider adjusts the overall image brightness so that the image appears to have been exposed correctly. Drag the slider to the left to darken the image and to the right to brighten it.

- **Recovery.** One of the problems frequently encountered with digital capture is overexposure. If the image is overexposed (as a result of incorrect camera settings), the Recovery slider can be used to coax details out of its highlights (the brightest part of the image).

- **Fill Light.** In traditional photography, a fill light is used to open up areas of shadow. It is not the key or dominant light source but a complementary light source. In the same way, the Fill Light slider works to brighten details within shadows without brightening the deepest blacks.

- **Blacks.** This slider makes a significant change in the darkest shadows with much less change in the midtones and highlights. As a result, increasing the blacks can increase the contrast in an image. When adjusting the Blacks slider, be careful not to increase its value so much that there is great loss of detail in the dark tones of the image.

(continued on next page)

Reset Sliders to Their Defaults

Here's a handy time-saving tip: Reset any slider in Camera Raw to its default position by double-clicking it.

Reveal Clipping in Camera Raw

The tone sliders constitute an amazing set of adjustments, but you can overuse them. To see how far you can push the Exposure, Recovery, or Blacks values without producing negative results, hold down Alt (Windows) Option (Mac) while adjusting these sliders to preview where highlights or shadows are clipped. By doing this, you can drag the slider until clipping begins, and then reverse the adjust-ment slightly. On the other hand, you can click on trian-gles on the top left and right of the histogram to toggle the clipping indicators on/off.

- **Brightness.** Similar to the Exposure slider, the Brightness slider adjusts the brightness and darkness of the image. However, this slider does not clip (or lose) the image highlights or shadows as aggressively as the Exposure slider. For this reason, it's best to first set the overall tonal scale using the Exposure, Recovery, and Blacks sliders, and then set the brightness. Brightness adjustments also can affect shadow or highlight clipping, so after making a Brightness adjustment, verify and/or readjust the Exposure, Recovery, or Blacks settings as needed.

- **Contrast.** After you have set the Exposure, Blacks, and Brightness val-ues, you need to set the contrast. The Contrast slider mainly affects the midtones (although it affects the darktones and highlights some-what). When you increase contrast, the middle-to-dark image areas become darker, and the middle-to-light image areas become lighter.

- **Clarity.** This setting adds depth and sharpness to an image by increas-ing local contrast. (You can think of sharpness and contrast as birds of a feather.) When using this setting, it is best to zoom in to 100% or greater. To maximize the effect, increase the setting until you see halos near the edge details of the image, and then reduce the setting slightly.

Tip
For even more information about adjusting photos in Camera Raw, visit http://tv.adobe.com and do a search for Camera Raw.

As you begin to work more with these and the other Camera Raw controls, you'll soon discover that it would be helpful to process multiple images simultaneously. This approach is especially useful when you have images that were taken under similar conditions.

1. In Adobe Bridge, select multiple files and open them in Camera Raw. Thumbnails of your selected images will appear in a vertical-column—the Filmstrip pane—on the left side of the Camera Raw window (**Figure 30b**).

2. Click the Select All button to select all the images. Now when you modify any of the Camera Raw controls, the modification will be applied to all the images. Or, you can select a single image and make adjustments. Click the Select All button, and then click the

Synchronize button to open the Synchronize dialog box where you can determine which adjustments will be applied (**Figure 30c**).

Figure 30b When you open multiple images at one time, they appear in the Filmstrip pane.

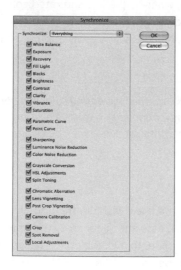

Figure 30c Use the Synchronize dialog box to choose which adjustments you would like to synchronize.

Tip
If you would like to learn more about adjusting multiple images, you can watch a free video tutorial on this topic at http://tv.adobe.com.

Save Photoshop Camera Raw Settings

As you develop your Camera Raw workflow, you may discover that you tend to use specific adjustments over and over again. In this case, saving those adjustments as a preset can be a real time-saver. Open the Camera Raw Settings menu (click the icon in the upper right of the image adjustment tab area) and choose Save Settings. There are also a number of resources where you can download or purchase prebuilt Camera Raw settings, such as http://getit.davidjay.com.

Copy and Paste Settings

You can also use Bridge to apply Camera Raw settings to multiple files by copying and pasting:

1. In Bridge, select an image that has been edited in Camera Raw.

2. Choose Edit > Develop Settings > Copy Camera Raw Settings.

3. Select one or more files, and then choose Edit > Develop Settings > Paste Settings.

#31 Enhancing Color with Vibrance and Saturation

Add Color Variety with Vibrance

The Vibrance slider has many uses; one of my favorites is to increase the Vibrance value to add color variety. I have found this to be especially effective when working on images of fall leaves, sunsets, and sepia-toned images, to name a few.

If you want to add a subtle color improvement and at the same time add more color variety, try decreasing the Saturation slider and increasing the Vibrance slider.

Creative Color

Try experimenting with the Saturation and Vibrance sliders in unison with the other Camera Raw color controls. For example, try creating a unique "antique effect" by decreasing the saturation and increasing the color temperature, thus making the image more yellow.

The Vibrance and Saturation sliders are located at the bottom of the Basic tab (**Figure 31**).

Figure 31 Increase Vibrance to boost less saturated colors. Increase Saturation to boost all color.

By thinking of these settings as teammates, your image enhancements will be better than ever. Both are useful for increasing and decreasing color saturation, yet each creates a different effect. Let's look a little deeper into the strengths and weaknesses of each.

Vibrance

The Vibrance slider is excellent for making nonlinear color adjustments. It analyzes the color in an image, and rather than affecting all the colors in a uniform way, it treats different colors in different ways. For example, if you increase the Vibrance slider, the bright and highly saturated colors will remain relatively unmodified, whereas the less-saturated colors will become more colorful—in essence, brighter and more varied. If you decrease the Vibrance slider, the weaker colors fade away and only the most prominent colors remain.

Tip
The Vibrance slider is especially effective when increasing color in a portrait photograph because of the way it handles skin tones. The tool has built-in logic, which prevents oversaturation of skin tones when vibrancy is increased.

Saturation

The Saturation slider modifies color in a linear fashion, treating all the colors in an image equally. If you decrease the slider to 0, the image turns to grayscale. If you increase the slider to 100, the image becomes oversaturated, and some colors will be clipped (leading to a loss of detail).

#32 Using the Tone Curve

It is best to make initial tone adjustments in the Basic tab, and then switch to the Tone Curve tab to fine-tune your images. There are two methods of making tone curve adjustments: Parametric and Point. Each has its own tab within the Tone Curve tab. Both let you make changes to the tonal scale of an image. This tonal scale is displayed on the horizontal axis with the dark tones on the left and the bright tones on the right.

Parametric tone curve

The Parametric tab is divided into four quadrants: Highlights, Lights, Darks, or Shadows (**Figure 32a**). Use the sliders to increase or decrease the darkness or brightness of a particular quadrant. If you would like more specific control, the quadrants can be expanded or contracted by dragging the Region Divider controls along the horizontal axis of the graph.

Figure 32a The tone curve in the Parametric tab.

Point tone curve

The Point tab is also divided into four quadrants (**Figure 32b**). However, the modifications are not confined to the quadrant. To make a modification, simply click and drag a point on the curve in the Point tab. Drag the point up to increase brightness. Drag the point down to decrease brightness.

Photoshop Curves vs. Camera Raw Curves

Curves in Photoshop and Camera Raw look similar but act differently. While working in Camera Raw, it is best to change perspectives and think about curves as a way to modify tone as opposed to the ability to modify tone and individual color channels in Photoshop Curves.

Figure 32b The tone curve in the Point tab.

The Point tab is supplied with presets, which you access via the Curve menu. Try the Medium Contrast (default setting), because it will increase contrast and color saturation.

Note
The changes you make in the Point tab are not reflected in the Parametric tab.

#33 Adjusting Hue, Saturation, and Luminance

The sliders on the HSL/Grayscale tab allow you to make adjustments to a specific range of color. With these controls, you can boost the level of one color relative to others or increase and decrease saturation and luminance (**Figure 33a**).

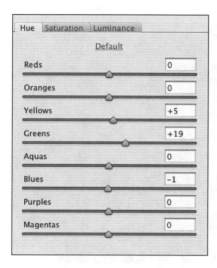

Figure 33a The Hue, Saturation, and Luminance tabs are nested within the HSL/Grayscale tab.

Each of the HSL tabs controls one aspect of color, and each slider on each tab controls the characteristics of a single color range:

- **Hue.** The fundamental nature of a color within a limited range. In other words, you cannot change a blue to red, but you can change blue from cyan to purple.

- **Saturation.** The vividness of a color. For instance, you can change a blue sky from gray (no color) to highly saturated blue.

- **Luminance.** The brightness of the color range.

To get a better handle on HSL, let's consider the following scenario: You have created a beautiful landscape photograph. The image is good, but you want to enhance the blue sky color. How would you do it?

1. Click the Hue tab and drag the Blues slider to dial in the exact shade of blue you want.

2. Click the Saturation tab and drag the Blues slider to the right to increase the saturation of the blue tones in the image.

3. Click the Luminance tab and drag the Blues slider to the left to make the sky a deeper and darker blue (**Figure 33b**).

Figure 33b The color of the sky in the left half of this image was deepened using the HSL controls.

This scenario is a good example of times when you will utilize all three HSL tabs to produce the desired result. Other times, the best result will be produced by using just one HSL tab.

#34 Creating Black-and-White Images

Creating stunning black-and-white images is now easier than ever using Camera Raw. If you haven't worked with black and white, now is the time. You can apply an automatic grayscale conversion by selecting the Convert to Grayscale option at the top of the HSL/Grayscale tab (**Figure 34a**).

Figure 34a Select Convert to Grayscale to make a custom grayscale conversion.

Camera Raw makes its best guess at a good grayscale conversion based on the image's White Balance setting, and the Hue, Saturation, and Luminance tabs are replaced by a single Grayscale Mix tab. The sliders on this tab show the relative proportions of different colors in the image that Camera Raw chose to mix together to create the grayscale image.

Of course, you're not stuck with the choices made by Camera Raw. For the best results, use the Grayscale Mix sliders. Drag these sliders to make specific color ranges lighter or darker to determine the contribution of each color to the grayscale version of the image.

For example, in a photograph of my daughter Annika, I wanted to modify the tonality of her blue jean overalls. Because the overalls represent the only blue in the image, I was able to modify the tonality using the Blues slider on the Grayscale Mix tab. Dragging the slider to the left darkens the blue in her overalls (**Figure 34b**).

Software Safety Nets

Suppose you're fiddling with the sliders on the Grayscale Mix tab to create a custom black-and-white conversion, and you decide that you hate what you've come up with. Camera Raw provides two easy ways of starting over. Click Auto at the top of the tab to return to the automatic conversion that Camera Raw produced when you first selected Convert to Grayscale. Alternatively, click Default to reset all the sliders to their zero position.

Creating the Best Black and White

One of the advantages of using the Grayscale Mix sliders to create a black-and-white image is that they don't affect the overall tone, brightness, or contrast in the image. But sometimes you can improve your conversion by using the controls on the Basic and Tone Curve tabs as well.

Once you've adjusted the Grayscale Mix sliders, be sure to revisit the Basic and Tone Curve tabs to make final contrast and tone adjustments.

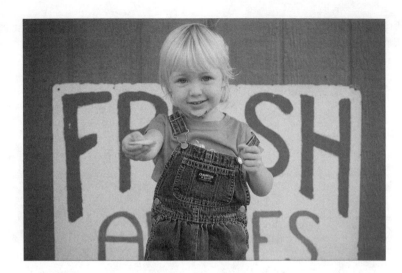

Figure 34b The Blues slider on the Grayscale Mix tab has been dragged to the left, resulting in the darker blue jean overalls.

Dragging the slider to the right has the opposite effect (**Figure 34c**).

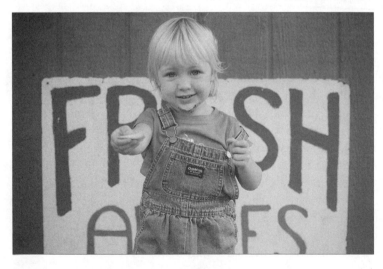

Figure 34c Dragging the Blues slider to the right lightens the overalls.

#35 Using Split Toning

To add color to a grayscale image (or tweak the color of a color image), use the controls in the Split Toning tab. Notice that the Split Toning tab has Hue and Saturation sliders for both Highlights and Shadows areas. The Balance slider lets you adjust the relative influence of the Highlights and Shadows controls (**Figure 35**).

Figure 35 Use the controls in the Split Toning tab to add color to both grayscale and color images.

Why Split Tone Color Images?

The primary intent of the Split Toning tab is to modify grayscale images. However, the Split Toning controls can be used to create special effects (like cross-processing) when used to modify color images.

In either the Highlights or Shadows area, start by dragging the Hue slider to select the color that you would like to add to the image. Then drag the Saturation slider to control the color intensity. If needed, drag the Balance slider to the right to increase the effect of the Highlights controls on the image; drag to the left to give the Shadows settings more prominence.

Sepia tone

You can add one color throughout the tonal range—to create a sepia tone effect, for example—by adjusting only the Highlights or Shadows sliders.

Split tone

To create a split tone image, you must adjust both the Highlights and Shadows sliders so that a different color is applied to the shadows and the highlights. Then you adjust the Balance slider to modify the intensity of the toning balance between the Highlights and Shadows controls.

Note
When using the Split Toning sliders, the added tone does not affect the extreme shadows and highlights; they remain black and white.

#36 Using Lens Corrections

The Lens Corrections tab is designed to give photographers a tool to fix common problems with photographic hardware, such as lens vignetting and chromatic aberration. However, this tab also provides creative photographic controls that go well beyond the simple functionality of fixing problems.

Fixing lens vignetting

Vignetting is a lens defect that occurs with certain lenses (especially wide angle lenses), causing the edges and especially the corners of an image to be darker. In many instances, especially in architectural photography, the result of lens vignetting is undesirable. You can use the Lens Vignetting sliders to compensate or remove the vignetting (**Figure 36a**).

Figure 36a Use the controls on the Lens Corrections tab for creative results or to fix lens vignetting or chromatic aberration.

Drag the Amount slider to the right to lighten the corners or drag to the left to darken the corners.

Use the Midpoint slider to expand or contract the vignetting effect. For example, you might drag the Amount slider to the left to darken the corners. Then you might decrease the Midpoint value to increase the "reach" of the vignetting so that the darkening extends from the corners toward the center of the image. Conversely, you could increase the Midpoint value to restrict the darkening adjustment to an area closer to the corners.

Adding creative lens vignetting

Many photographers are now using the Lens Vignetting and Post Crop Vignetting controls to darken the corners of images (**Figure 36b**). In previous versions of Camera Raw you could only add a vignette if the image had not been cropped. New to Camera Raw CS4 are the Post Crop Vignetting controls, which allow you to brighten/darken the edges of your photo. In addition, you can control the shape and edge of the effect with the Roundness and Feather controls. Either way, whatever controls you use, modifying the edge of your photo adds a unique look and feel. Adding a lens vignette will affect the overall tone of an image. Thus, once you have applied the effect, be sure to go back to the Basic and Tone Curve tabs to make final tone adjustments.

Figure 36b This photograph was taken on a recent surf trip to Baja, Mexico. The lens vignetting was added in Camera Raw by decreasing the Amount and Midpoint values.

Correcting chromatic aberration

Chromatic aberration is a lens defect that results in images with *color fringing*, in which the details near the corners of an image have a red or cyan fringe. To identify chromatic aberration, zoom in to an area near the corner of an image and look for color fringing. While color fringing isn't all that common, except when using wide angle lenses, it's worth noting how to fix it in case you encounter it.

In the Camera Raw Lens Corrections tab, adjust either of the Fix Red/ Cyan Fringe or Fix Blue/Yellow Fringe sliders. As you adjust these controls to the left and right, watch the fringe in the image increase or decrease until you find the correct setting. The goal is to remove as much of the color fringing as possible.

Tip

When adjusting one of the Chromatic Aberration sliders, press and hold Alt (Windows) Option (Mac) to hide fringes of other colors. This way you can focus in on the color fringing that you are attempting to fix.

#37 Using the Spot Removal and Red Eye Removal Tools

Camera Raw is equipped with the Spot Removal tool, which is very effective at general retouching. You can use it to remove or reduce unwanted distractions, blemishes, dust, scratches, and so on. The advantage of retouching in Camera Raw, as opposed to retouching in Photoshop, is that it is nondestructive and doesn't drastically increase your file size. On the other hand, keep in mind that it's better to perform fine retouching in Photoshop, since that program provides more detail control.

To begin retouching in Camera Raw, follow these steps:

1. Choose the Spot Healing tool on the Camera Raw toolbar and choose from the Type menu the kind of retouching you want to do: Heal or Clone (see the sidebar "Clone and Heal in Camera Raw") (**Figure 37a**).

Figure 37a Choose the Spot Removal tool and then choose Heal or Clone.

2. Move the Radius slider to the right or left to increase or decrease the area affected by the tool.

3. Move the Opacity slider to the left to create a more transparent retouch.

4. In the image, click the spot to be retouched. Two circles will appear: A red circle shows the area being retouched, and the green circle indicates the source area for retouching.

5. To reposition either circle, simply drag within it. To increase or decrease the size of either circle, hover over the circle edge until the cursor becomes a double arrow, and then drag (**Figure 37b**).

Clone and Heal in Camera Raw

The Camera Raw Heal and Clone tools work identically to the Healing and Cloning tools in Photoshop. Both tools sample and copy pixels to another area in the image. The main difference between the tools is that the Healing tool carefully blends the texture of the copied area (the source) with the pixels in the area being retouched, whereas the Clone tool copies and pastes pixels from the source with a feathered version of the sampled area.

Area being retouched indicated by red circle

Source area indicated by green circle

Figure 37b Resize the Retouch tool by dragging the edge of either circle. You can also drag either circle to reposition it.

Red eye removal

Most cameras today come equipped with a red-eye reduction flash setting. However, this feature doesn't always do the trick, especially when using small point-and-shoot cameras whose flash units are very close to their lenses.

To remove red eye using Camera Raw:

1. Choose the Red Eye Removal tool from the toolbar (**Figure 37c**).

Figure 37c The Red Eye Removal tool.

2. Drag a rectangle around the eye. It is best to create a rectangle that is slightly bigger than the iris (**Figure 37d**).

(continued on next page)

Using Photoshop Camera Raw

Figure 37d Drag to create a rectangle a bit bigger than the iris of the eye.

3. When you release the mouse button, the selection will reduce to the size of the red area (**Figure 37e**).

Figure 37e The red area is selected.

4. Modify the Pupil and Darken sliders to fine-tune the correction.

Repeat these steps for the other eye(s) that needs correction.

#38 Making Localized Adjustments

New to Camera Raw in CS4 is the ability to make adjustments, corrections, and enhancements to specific areas of the images. In contrast, in the previous versions, most corrections had to be made to the entire image. The Photoshop team took this limitation into consideration and provided an amazing solution with the Adjustment Brush and Graduated Filter (#39). And as you'll soon discover, you will use these tools on a regular basis.

Start by selecting the Adjustment Brush tool (**Figure 38a**). Camera Raw will open the tool options under the histogram (**Figure 38b**). By default the mask mode is set to New, so that you can create a new adjustment. Modify the controls by dragging the sliders to define the type of adjustment you would like to make. Drag to the right to increase or to the left to decrease the particular adjustment. The following list describes what the different controls affect.

Adjustment Brush (K)

Figure 38a To select the Adjustment Brush tool, click the appropriate icon or press K.

Figure 38b The Adjustment Brush options.

- **Exposure.** Adjusts the overall image brightness with a stronger effect on the brighter tones.

- **Brightness.** Adjusts the image brightness with a greater effect in the midtones.

- **Contrast.** Adjusts the image contrast with a greater effect in the midtones.

- **Saturation.** Modifies the overall color intensity.

- **Clarity.** Adds subtle dimension or depth to an image by increasing local contrast.

- **Sharpness.** Changes the edge definition and details of the image.

- **Color.** Enables you to add a color tint (not a color change) to a specific area.

Tip

In addition to dragging the slider, you can also click the plus icon (+) or the minus icon (−) multiple times to increase or decrease the adjustment. Many times, while you are making an adjustment, you will discover that you have modified the control too far. In those situations, simply double-click the slider to reset the effect to zero.

After you have set the controls, the next step is to specify the brush options. Here it is helpful to position the brush over the image to see the current Brush settings (**Figure 38c**).

Don't Forget to Zoom

If you decide to use an extremely low Feather amount, the solid circle may not be visible. This is not a problem, but it does typically result from being zoomed out to far. When you are correcting areas that require a small brush, be sure to zoom in so you can see and make an even better adjustment.

Undo Adjustments

With any type of brush work, at some point you will almost always need to undo what you've done. Press Ctrl + Z (Windows) Command + Z (Mac) to undo your last adjustment. Or to undo part of the adjustment, click Erase in the Adjustment Brush tool options and paint over the adjustment. On the other hand, if you need to remove the entire adjustment, select the pin and press Delete.

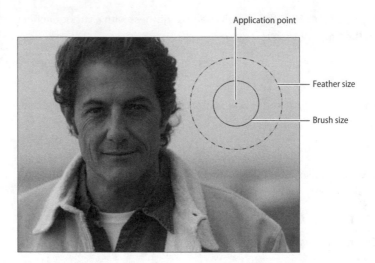

Application point

Feather size

Brush size

Figure 38c The Adjustment Brush visuals reveal the brush size and feather. The farther away the two circles are from each other, the stronger the feathering amount.

- **Size.** Controls the overall diameter of the brush.

- **Feather.** Controls the softness or hardness of the brush stroke.

- **Flow.** Controls the rate of application.

- **Density.** Controls the overall intensity (or more technically the transparency) of the stroke.

- **Auto Mask.** Limits the brush stroke to an area of similar color and tone.

Next, paint with the Adjustment Brush onto the area that you want to correct (**Figure 38d**). When you paint, you'll notice a pin icon, which shows you the initial application point. If the pin is distracting, press the H key to hide/show the icon. For even more precision, select the Show Mask option to reveal the area being adjusted. To change the color of the Mask overlay, click on the color chip to the right of the words Show Mask and choose a new color.

Before - Dark shadows around eyes   After - Shadows have been reduced

Figure 38d The original (left) image is corrected (right) by painting in an increased exposure. This correction was needed to remove shadows that appeared around the eyes as a result of improper lighting. The final result is a more compelling portrait.

Tip

As you will discover, the Adjustment Brush is a bit tricky. Therefore, don't miss out on a great learning resource—a free video tutorial on making localized adjustments is at http://tv.adobe.com.

#**39** Using the Graduated Filter Tool

The Graduated Filter is another *very* welcome new tool to Camera Raw CS4. This tool is based on a traditional photographic filter that helped photographers achieve correct exposure. In the same way, you can use this filter to make localized adjustments to specific areas of your image. While the Graduate Filter can be used make a wide range of adjustments (Exposure, Brightness, Contrast, Saturation, Clarity, Sharpness, Color), it is most typically used to darken bright areas of sky or to brighten dark areas of the foreground.

For starters, think of the Graduated Filter as a cousin to the Adjustment Brush (#38) because they both have similar controls. To use the Graduated Filter, click its icon on the toolbar or press G (**Figure 39a**). The options will appear under the histogram (**Figure 39b**).

Graduated Filter (G)

Figure 39a To select the tool, click the appropriate icon or press G.

Figure 39b The Graduated Filter options.

Next, choose the type of adjustment you want to make in the Graduated Filter tool options by dragging the slider for any of the listed effects. After you have defined the adjustment, click and drag in the image.

Once you have dragged on the image, you'll notice the overlay visuals, which show you where and how the adjustment will be made (**Figure 39c**). The green dot represents the start point at the beginning edge of the filter. The red dot represents the center of the ending edge of the filter. The black-and-white dotted line connecting the points represents the midline. The green-and-white and red-and-white dotted lines represent the beginning and end of the range of the effect.

Before - Bright sky

Starting point (green)

After - Darkened sky
Middle (black and white)
Ending edge (red)

Figure 39c A Graduated Filter correction has been applied to the bottom image so that the sky is darker and more visually interesting. In addition, you can view the overlay graphics, which depict where the adjustment occurs.

Tip
The Graduated Filter overlay graphics help you visualize where the effect starts and stops. But if the overlay becomes distracting, press V to hide/show it.

Traditional Photography and the Graduated Filter

As I briefly mentioned, the Graduated Filter has its roots in a traditional photographic filter. This filter was a shaded piece of glass that gradually faded from top to bottom. Ultimately, it helped landscape photographers have a correct exposure for the land and the bright sky. In fact, the filter works very similar to the shading that you find in most car windshields. Typically, car windshields are shaded at the top to prevent a driver from being overwhelmed by the brightness of the sky. So why do I bring this up? Well, my hope is that by knowing how the traditional filter worked, it can help you begin to identify and correct this age-old photographic problem in your images.

#**40** Cropping, Rotating, and Straightening

The advantage of cropping, rotating, and straightening in Camera Raw is simple: What would be destructive in Photoshop can be done non-destructively in Camera Raw. The ability to reconstruct the image to its precropped, rotated, or straightened state provides a creative "safety net" that is helpful for amateurs and pros alike.

Cropping and rotating

To crop an image in Camera Raw:

1. Open an image in Camera Raw. Click and hold on the Crop tool to choose a preset aspect ratio for your crop area. You can also use this menu to clear a current crop.

2. To define a crop area, drag out a rectangle around the area that you want to preserve. The part of the image that will be cropped is grayed out (**Figure 40a**).

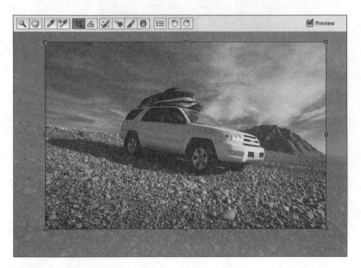

Figure 40a Drag a rectangle around the area you want to keep.

3. To modify the size of the crop, drag any of the middle or corner anchor points.

4. To reposition the crop area, click anywhere inside it and drag.

5. When you are finished with your crop, press Enter (Windows) Return (Mac) to view the results.

Note

Being able to view the crop is a brand-new feature in CS4. Previously, you had to return to Bridge or open the image in Photoshop to view the crop. While this new feature won't make anyone's top ten list, it is one of those gems that's worth its weight in gold!

Straightening

An important element of a photograph is a level horizon line. The Straighten tool can help you level or straighten your image in no time at all. Choose the Straighten tool on the toolbar and drag along an object in the image that should be level. This will automatically rotate and crop the image so that the line that you created is straight (**Figure 40b**).

Figure 40b Drag with the Straighten tool along a line that should be horizontal.

Tip

While in Camera Raw, press Ctrl (Windows) Command (Mac) to temporarily select the Straighten tool.

Arbitrary Rotation

You can also arbitrarily rotate an image using the Crop tool:

1. Create a crop area as described in the section "Cropping and rotating."

2. Move the cursor toward one of the four corner points of the crop. When you see the cursor change appearance so that it has two arrows, drag to rotate the crop area.

If You Change Your Mind

You can clear the crop area or cancel a rotation or straightening operation at any time by pressing the Esc key.

#41 Sharpening and Reducing Noise

The Sharpening and Noise Reduction controls are located on the Detail tab (**Figure 41**).

Figure 41 The Detail tab.

To achieve the best results with these controls, be sure to change your zoom level to 100%. Choose the zoom level from the menu on the lower left of the Camera Raw window.

Tip
The quickest way to change your zoom to 100% is to double-click the Zoom tool on the toolbar.

Sharpening

The type and intensity of sharpening that you apply is contingent upon the image. Because of the many variations in photographs, sharpening is more of an art than a formula. To sharpen effectively, you need to learn about the basic principles, and then apply those to a particular image. In Camera Raw, the Sharpening sliders affect only the luminosity information in the image—that is, the light and dark values of each pixel. Color information is not changed.

Typically, it is best to begin your adjustments using the Amount and Radius sliders on the Detail tab, which control how much sharpening is applied to the entire image and how it is applied. Then move on to the Detail and Masking sliders to dial back the sharpening in certain areas:

- **Amount slider.** Adjusts edge definition. A value of zero equals zero sharpening. Increase the Amount value to sharpen the whole image. Typically, it is best to set a lower value for this control, because high values tend to create "halos," or visible artifacts, around sharpened areas.

- **Radius slider.** Adjusts the size of the details to which the sharpening is applied. The correct Radius setting will depend on the image. If you have an image with fine details, try a lower radius setting; if your image is dominated by large objects, try a higher radius.

- **Detail slider.** Tones down the halos added by the Amount slider while keeping edges sharp. A setting of 0 gets rid of halos almost entirely, and a setting of 100 preserves them. For blurry images, try a lower setting. To emphasize texture, try a higher setting.

- **Masking slider.** Applies a mask to the sharpening that protects relatively smooth areas that don't need much sharpening and concentrates the sharpening along the edges of items. (I'll talk about masks in Chapter 5, "Working with Layers," but for the moment just remember that in Photoshop a mask is a technique for protecting part of an image from editing, like masking tape). With a Masking slider setting of zero, everything in the image receives an equal amount of sharpening. With a setting of 100, sharpening is mostly limited to the strongest edges.

Noise reduction

The Noise Reduction sliders can be used to improve images that have noise (visible artifacts that degrade the image). Noise often occurs as a result of shooting with a high ISO, improper exposure, or a low-quality digital capture. These sliders are not a cure-all for noise, but for many of us they are a regular step in our photographic workflow.

Drag the Luminance slider to the right to reduce grayscale noise. This will smooth out the irregular shape and size of noise. Drag the Color slider to the right to reduce color noise. Typically, the default Color Noise amount of 25 will be more than sufficient. In fact, most of the time it's

Advanced Sharpening

While adjusting any of the Sharpening sliders, hold down Alt (Windows) Option (Mac) to get a grayscale display of the results of your work. However, what is displayed is not the same for each slider:

- When dragging the Amount slider, the grayscale image shows the full effect on the Luminosity channel of all the sharpening adjustments you've made.

- Dragging the Radius or Detail slider reveals the degree to which the image is being sharpened (dark areas are sharpened more, light areas less).

- The grayscale image displayed when dragging the Masking slider shows the actual mask applied to the image in which black corresponds to no sharpening and white corresponds to sharpening.

best to choose an amount below 25. When reducing noise, be careful not to increase the settings so high as to oversoften the image. If the image does become soft, be sure to increase the overall sharpening amounts. In fact, that's why the Noise Reduction and Sharpening controls are located in the same panel!

Tip

If an image has a high amount of noise, using Noise Reduction in Camera Raw is a good starting point. If you need to reduce noise further, try the Reduce Noise Filter in Photoshop or one of the many noise reduction plug-ins that you can purchase separately.

CHAPTER FIVE

Working with Layers

Layers are integral to working in Photoshop. They allow you to keep image elements and adjustments separate from one another so that you can move them independently and enable or disable them at will. You can think of layers as sheets of clear transparent film stacked one on top of the other.

Here's a quick example of how layers work: Say you have a single layer Photoshop document that contains an image, and you want to add text on top of the image. To do this, you choose the Type tool and click within the document window. This adds a type layer above the image. The result is a document that contains two layers: The bottom layer contains the image, and the top layer contains the type. Each of these layers can be dealt with individually.

Layers can be used for a wide array of tasks, such as compositing multiple images, adding text to an image, adding vector graphics, making color and tone adjustments, converting an image to black and white, adding special effects to an image, and more. The advantage of a layers-based workflow is that you can make edits nondestructively. For example, if you're using a color image as the background layer, you can add an adjustment layer to convert that background layer to black and white. This type of edit is nondestructive because it is not permanent. If you decide that you don't like the black-and-white adjustment, you can simply hide or delete the layer, or edit the settings.

Because layers are essential to nondestructive image editing, you should strive to become adept at using them. Layers are an integral part of a sound photographic workflow. Getting into the habit of using them can help you work more efficiently with more creative results.

#42 Using the Layers Panel

The Layers panel displays the layer structure of your Photoshop file. It also includes controls for manipulating layers, including creating new ones and deleting old ones, changing the layer stacking order, changing the visibility of layers, collecting layers into groups, and adding layer effects.

To view the Layers panel, choose Window > Layers or press F7 (**Figure 42a**).

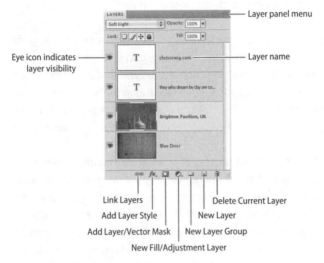

Figure labels: Layer panel menu, Eye icon indicates layer visibility, Layer name, Link Layers, Add Layer Style, Add Layer/Vector Mask, New Fill/Adjustment Layer, New Layer Group, New Layer, Delete Current Layer

Figure 42a The Layers panel.

The buttons located along the bottom of the panel perform these functions:

- **Link Layers.** Links two or more layers. When one linked layer is repositioned or transformed, all linked layers are simultaneously repositioned or transformed.

- **Add Layer Style.** Creates a variety of effects, such as shadows, glows, and bevels, that change the appearance of a layer. Layer effects are linked to the layer contents.

- **Add Layer Mask.** Creates a mask that can be used to show or hide portions of the layer and reveal the layers below. Masking layers is a valuable technique for combining multiple photos into a single image or for making local color and tonal corrections.

Background Information

Most Photoshop images start off with a single layer called *Background*. This layer has very special properties: It can't have any transparent pixels, its opacity can't be adjusted, it can't be moved (either dragged within the image frame or by restacking), and its blending mode can't be changed.

But it's easy to convert the Background into a normal layer: Double-click it in the Layers panel to open the New Layer dialog box. Type a name for the converted layer in the Name field and click OK.

Duplicating Layers

If you want to try out some edits on an image, but you want to preserve the original, make a duplicate of the layer you're working on first. Select the layer (or Background) and press Ctrl + J (Windows) Command + J (Mac).

- **New Adjustment Layer.** Adds an adjustment layer to the image, which allows you to edit color and tone nondestructively (see the next how-to for more information).

- **New Layer Group.** Organizes selected layers by placing them in a folder.

- **New Layer.** Creates a new layer above the currently targeted layer. To create a layer below the currently selected layer, press Ctrl (Windows) Command (Mac) while clicking the New Layer button.

- **Delete Current Layer.** Deletes the currently selected layer(s).

You can toggle the visibility of layers on or off by clicking the Eye icon to the left of a specific layer. Rename a layer by double-clicking its name (in the Layers panel) and then typing.

Layers are indispensable when creating composite images, such as the one shown in **Figure 42b**, which illustrates the combination of text and image layers shown in Figure 42a.

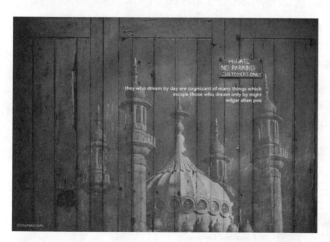

Figure 42b The image that results from the combination of the layers shown in Figure 42a.

Worried About Layers and File Size?

If you're new to using layers, you may be concerned about creating too many layers and unnecessarily increasing the file size. While this is a valid concern—you always need to be concerned about file size—keep in mind that layers expand your creative potential. In many cases, the benefits you gain by expanding and experimenting with layers far outweigh the extra file size.

Fun Fact

How many layers can be created in one Photoshop document? The layer limit per document is a whopping 8,000 layers!

#**43** Creating Adjustment Layers

Chapter 9, "Modifying Color and Tone," introduces you to the various commands on the Adjustments submenu (Image > Adjustments) that you'll use to alter the tone and color characteristics of your pictures. There's one problem with those commands, though: Their effects are permanent. They change the actual pixels in your image, and if you change your mind later, you're stuck (unless you use the Undo command immediately, of course).

Now, one of the most celebrated aspects of digital photography is flexibility, and adjustment layers provide this in spades. Adjustment layers apply color and tonal adjustments to your image nondestructively; that is, without permanently changing pixel values. The advantages of nondestructive adjustments are twofold: First, they give you the ability to undo or remove an adjustment and restore the image to its original state. Second, the ability to undo can act as a safety net, which allows for more creative experimentation.

To create a new adjustment layer, do one of the following:

- Choose Layer > New Adjustment Layer, and then choose an option. Name the layer, set layer options, and click OK.

- Click the Create New Adjustment Layer icon at the bottom of the Layers panel and choose a type of adjustment layer from the menu (**Figure 43a**). The dialog box for the particular adjustment you chose displays.

- Click the Adjustments panel tab to target the panel (or if it is closed, double-click the Adjustments panel tab to expand the panel, and then click an adjustment icon or one of the presets below (**Figure 43b**).

Figure 43a Click the Create New Adjustment Layer icon to open the menu showing the available types of adjustment layers.

Adjustment panel menu

Switch between Standard and Expanded views

Click to determine if adjustments clip to layer or affect all layers below

Figure 43b The Adjustments panel is a great new feature in Photoshop CS4 because it provides you with an easier way to access and modify your adjustments.

At first glance, the Adjustment Layer icons are a bit hard to decipher. Hover the cursor over an icon to display the adjustment in the top left of the panel. Or view **Figure 43c**, which provides a key to make learning the icons much easier.

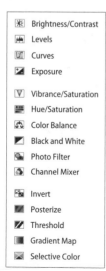

Figure 43c The Adjustments panel icons.

Modifying Adjustment Layers

You can reopen the Settings dialog box for an adjustment layer by double-clicking the adjustment layer thumbnail in the Layers panel. This allows you to change the layer settings after you've created it.

Adjustment layers have many of the same properties as other layers. For example, you can turn their visibility on and off to apply their effect or to preview the effect. Or try lowering the opacity of an adjustment layer to lower the intensity of the effect.

Adjustment Layers and Masking

Adjustment layers have built-in layer masks that give you the ability to use the paint or fill tools to specify what part of the image will be modified. For more on masking, read Chapter 10, "Masking."

#44 Working with Multiple Layers

As you started to discover in the previous how-to, being able to work with multiple layers provides you with an incredible amount of flexiblity. It allows you to makes changes to your images on new layers and in that way make nondestructive edits—not to mention all the amazing things you can do with color, tone, and blending (more on that later!).

At times, you will want to create a new blank layer onto which you will add content. To create a new layer, do one of the following:

- Click the Create New Layer icon in the Layers panel or choose New Layer from the Layers panel menu (**Figure 44a**).

Figure 44a Creating a new layer.

- Choose Layer > New > Layer

- Shift + Ctrl + N (Windows) Shift + Command + N (Mac) to create a new layer and open the New Layer dialog box (**Figure 44b**).

- Shift + Alt + Ctrl + N (Windows) Shift + Option + Command + N (Mac) to create a new layer without opening the New Layer dialog box.

New Layer

Name: [   ] (OK)

☐ Use Previous Layer to Create Clipping Mask (Cancel)

Color: [☐ None ▲▼]

Mode: [Normal ▲▼] Opacity: [100 ▼] %

☐ (No neutral color exists for Normal mode.)

Figure 44b The New Layer dialog box.

At other times, you may need to duplicate the current layer. To duplicate a layer, do one of the following:

- Choose Layer > Duplicate Layer
- Click and drag the layer to the New Layer icon in the Layers panel.
- Press Ctrl + J (Windows) Command + J (Mac)

Once you have multiple layers, things can get tricky because it is possible to accidentally make changes that you did not intend to make. Fortunately, after you have made revisions to a layer, you can lock the layer (fully or partially) to protect its contents. Select the layer and click one of the layer locking icons located near the top of the Layers panel (**Figure 44c**).

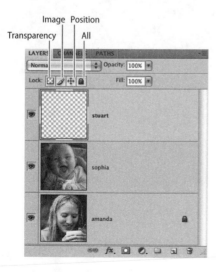

Figure 44c Layer-locking options.

Locked or Not Locked?

When a layer is locked, a lock icon appears to the right of the layer name. The lock icon is solid when the layer is fully locked and hollow when the layer is partially locked.

Speedy Layer Selection

As you start to get the hang of working with multiple layers, you'll soon discover the desire to quickly select or target a layer to make changes. You can of course select a layer in the Layers panel. But here's a tip that will make your life with layers even better. Position the cursor over the content of the layer you want to target. Next, right-click (Windows) Control-click (Mac) and a context menu will appear showing you all the layer names that are under your cursor. Select the layer name of the layer you want to target.

You can choose from the following options in the Layers panel:

- **Transparency.** Preserves transparency by confining editing to the opaque portions of the layer.

- **Image.** Protects the layer's pixels by preventing modification with the painting tools.

- **Position.** Prevents the layer's pixels from being moved.

- **All.** Completely locks the layer from any type of editing.

When is it best to use layer locking? It depends on the image. If there are a large number of detailed layers, you will find it helpful to lock a layer fully once it is complete. In other scenarios, you may want to lock a layer partially if it has the correct transparency and image but you are uncertain of the final positioning. Locking transparency is especially helpful if you want to add something to a layer that has transparency without affecting the underlying layers.

#45 Organizing with Layer Groups

I recently completed a layered composite image of one of the fastest cyclists in the world: Ivan Basso of the Trek Discovery Team. I was really excited about the image, so I put a lot of work into it. When I was finished, I counted 57 layers!

The only way to organize a complex image like that is to use layer groups. Layer groups provide the capability to collect layers into folders. While not all images will have that many layers, just about every image can use some organization.

To create a new layer group using default options, do one of the following:

- Click the New Layer Group icon in the Layers panel ⬜ .

- Choose Layer > New > Group.

- Choose New Group from the Layers panel menu.

You may find it helpful to put similar layers in groups. For example, if you are retouching an image and you have multiple layers for clean up, multiple layers for enhancements, and multiple layers for color and tone adjustments, you might create layer groups named Clean Up, Enhance, and Color and Tone to organize and simplify your layers. Then, rather than having to scroll through numerous layers, you can click the group layer triangle icon to expand and collapse a particular folder (**Figure 45**).

Click to expand/collapse the layer group contents

Figure 45 In this Photoshop file, layers are gathered into groups by function. To see the contents of a layer group, click the triangle next to its folder icon.

New Layer Group Speed Tip

When creating a new layer group, you can use a short-cut that enables you to open a dialog box and define a few settings. Simply press and hold Alt (Windows) Option (Mac) while clicking the New Layer Group icon in the Layers panel to display the New Group dialog box where you can set your layer group options:

- **Name.** Specifies a name for the group.

- **Color.** Assigns a color to the group in the Layers panel. This is for organizational purposes only. It will not affect the color of the layer group contents.

- **Mode.** Specifies a blending mode for the group.

- **Opacity.** Specifies an opacity level for the group.

When you are finished making your selections, click OK.

#46 Using Auto-Align and Auto-Blend

Combining multiple exposures into one composite typically presents some challenges. In particular, exposure differences or lens distortion between source images may create seams or inconsistencies in the combined image. However, Auto-Align and Auto-Blend are two exciting features from Photoshop CS3 that have been further improved in Photoshop CS4 and will help you align and blend multiple images together.

Auto-Align lets you align two or more images that have similar content, whereas Auto-Blend lets you blend multiple images that have overlapping content to create a panoramic or an extended depth of field image. Together, these two features let you combine multiple exposures with ease and create the appearance of smooth transitions in the final images. These features are helpful for a wide range of photographic subject matter, such as architecture, people, panoramic landscapes, macro photography, and more.

To combine two exposures into one composite image using the Auto-Align and Auto-Blend commands:

1. Copy or place the images you want to combine into the same document, keeping each image in a separate layer (**Figures 46a, 46b, 46c**).

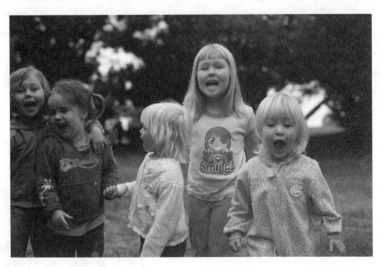

Figure 46a Original exposure 1.

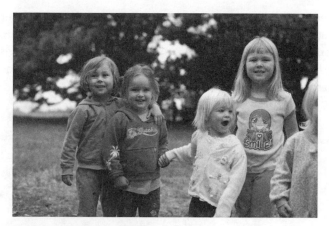

Figure 46b Original exposure 2.

Figure 46c The original images combined in the one document. Both layers are unlocked.

2. Select both layers by Ctrl-clicking (Windows) Command-clicking (Mac). Both layers are highlighted in the Layers panel.

3. Choose Edit > Auto-Align Layers. The Auto-Align Layers dialog box appears.

4. The Auto-Align Layers dialog box (**Figure 46d**) offers several Projection options for combining the images. For most images, select Auto. This will scale, transform geometrically, and position the images so that they are aligned.

Auto-Align Wide Angle Photographs

New to Photoshop CS4 is the ability to create a panoramic image from wide and more normal focal lengths. When combing wide angle photographs, be sure to turn on Vignette Removal to eliminate edge darkening that would prevent a successful image combination. Turn on Geometric Distortion to correct various types of distortion that occurs when using a wide angle lens or from being close to the subject with a more normal lens.

5. With the layers still selected, choose Edit > Auto-Blend Layers to open the Auto-Blend Layers dialog box (**Figure 46e**). Choose the Blend Method of Panorama. Here is where the final touch of magic happens: Photoshop applies layer masks as needed to each layer to produce a seamless composite image (**Figures 46f, 46g**).

Figure 46d Typically, the Auto option will provide the best results.

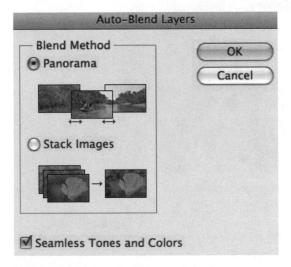

Figure 46e The Auto-Blend Layers dialog box.

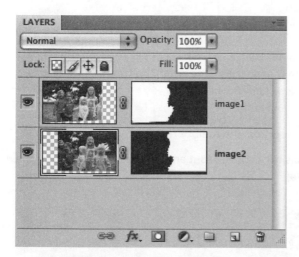

Figure 46f The Auto-Blend Layers command (Edit > Auto-Blend Layers) adds a layer mask to each layer base to seamlessly combine multiple layers.

Figure 46g The result of auto-alignment and auto-blending.

Note

For those of you who are a bit more advanced, try stacking your photos. Create a set of images that have the same subject and composition but have different focal points. Go through the preceding steps 1–5 except in step 5 choose Stack Images. Photoshop will build an image with extended depth of field.

Note

Auto-Blend Layers is only available for RGB or grayscale images.

#47 Using Type Layers

In Photoshop, text elements reside on their own layers, separate from bitmap image elements. A type layer is a vector layer (like a shape layer), so it can be scaled without losing any quality or detail. The type also remains editable, so you can change the words or other attributes (like typeface, font size, or font color) at any time.

To add text to an image:

1. Choose the Text tool from the Toolbox or press the T key.

2. From the options bar, choose a font and set the size and color of the font (**Figure 47a**).

     Font family   Font style   Font size   Type color

Toggle Character/Paragraph panels

Figure 47a With the Type tool active, the options bar displays commands for formatting text.

3. Click in the document window and start typing to add text—a new type layer is created automatically.

4. When you've finished entering text, press the Enter key on the numeric keypad to commit your changes to the type layer.

Edit text just like you would in a word processing document. Choose the Text tool and click anywhere within the text to place the insertion point. Either start typing to add new text or select existing text by double-clicking or by dragging (**Figure 47b**). Selected text can be replaced by typing or be reformatted by choosing new options from the options bar.

Figure 47b Selected text can be formatted or edited.

A wider range of text formatting options than you get in the options bar is available in the Character panel. Make sure a text layer is selected, and then click the Toggle Character/Paragraph panels icon on the options bar or choose Window > Character (**Figure 47c**).

Figure 47c For an exhaustive set of text formatting controls, use the Character panel.

Note

To perform certain operations on type, including applying some filters and painting with brushes, you must first rasterize the type layer. Rasterizing type converts it from vector art to pixel-based art (like ordinary photographic data), rendering the text uneditable. To rasterize type, select the type layer and choose Layer > Rasterize > Type.

Text Speed Tip

The quickest way to select and modify text is by way of the Layers panel. When you create a text layer, it is marked in the Layers panel with a "T" icon. Double-click the text layer icon "T" in the Layers panel to select all the text on that layer. Make any needed changes, and then press the Enter key on the numeric keypad to commit your changes.

#48 Using Layer Effects and Styles

In Photoshop, you'll find a whole arsenal of special *layer effects* that you can use to dress up the contents of a layer. These effects take the form of shadows, glows, three-dimensional appearances, overlays, and many more. You can apply more than one effect to a layer: All the effects applied to a layer taken together constitute a *layer style*.

Layer effects are linked to layers in the sense that they conform to the contents of the layer. For this reason, when you move or edit the layer, the effects adapt to the modified content. For example, if you add a Drop Shadow effect to a type layer, you can then edit the text or modify the characteristics of the font and the effect will be applied to the newly modified type. This flexibility makes layer effects and layer styles practical tools in anyone's workflow.

To create a layer style, start by adding a layer effect to a layer. Click the Add Layer Style icon at the bottom of the Layers panel and choose an effect from the menu (**Figure 48a**).

Figure 48a Click the Add Layer Style icon to choose a layer effect.

Add Layer Style icon

Choose one of the following effects:

- **Drop Shadow.** A shadow that appears behind and offset from the layer contents.

- **Inner Shadow.** A shadow that appears just inside the edges of the layer's content, giving the layer a hollowed-out appearance.

- **Outer Glow and Inner Glow.** Glows that project out from the content or hug the inside edges of the layer's content.

- **Bevel and Emboss.** Highlights and shadows that create a three-dimensional appearance.

- **Satin.** Interior shading that creates a smoothly textured finish.

- **Color, Gradient, and Pattern Overlay.** Overlays the layer content with a color, a gradient, or a pattern.

- **Stroke.** Draws an outline around the layer contents.

The Layer Style dialog box opens with the chosen layer effect selected (**Figure 48b**).

Figure 48b Choose options in the Layer Style dialog box for the selected effect. Click the check boxes next to the names of other effects to add those to the layer style.

To choose options for a layer style:

1. In the list on the left, add effects to the style by selecting the check boxes next to their names.

2. Click the name of a layer effect to access the options for that effect.

3. To apply the effect, click OK.

(continued on next page)

Quickly Copy Layer Styles

In certain instances, you will want to apply the same layer style to multiple layers. An example might be a document with five text layers that all need to have the same Stroke and Drop Shadow effects.

The most effective way to accomplish this is to apply the Stroke and Drop Shadow effects to one layer, and then copy the layer style to the remaining four layers.

In the Layers panel, press Alt (Windows) Option (Mac) and drag a single layer effect from one layer to another to another. To copy an entire layer style, hold Alt (Windows) Option (Mac) and drag the effects bar from one layer to another.

If you were to carry out either of these drag operations without holding down the modifier key, you would move the effect or layer style from one layer to another rather than duplicate it.

Create Layers from Layer Styles

Say that you've worked up an elaborate Photoshop file containing many layers using layer styles, and then you find that you need to use that image in an application that can't "read" Photoshop layer styles. You could flatten the image, but then you would lose all the flexibility that a layered image affords you.

If the target application supports Photoshop layers, there's a compromise solution available to you: You can separate each layer style into a stack of layers in which each layer effect is rasterized onto its own layer (see the note accompanying how-to #47 about rasterization). To do this, choose Layer > Layer Style > Create Layers to parse the various effects into separate layers.

In the Layers panel, the list of layer effects appears underneath the layer. Click the Eye icon to show or hide the effects. To the right of the layer name, the *fx* icon will show that one or more effects have been applied. Click the arrow on the far right to expand or collapse the list of effects (**Figure 48c**).

Figure 48c The *fx* icon indicates that effects have been applied to a layer. Click the arrow to the right of the *fx* icon to expand or collapse the view of the layer effects. Click the Eye icon to show or hide each effect.

Using layer styles can greatly enhance your work. In **Figure 48d**, I have applied Stroke and Drop Shadow effects to the type layers to help separate the text from the background image.

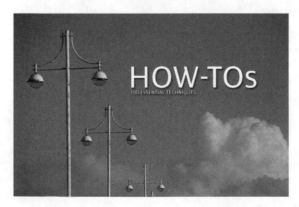

Figure 48d A layer style consisting of a stroke and a drop shadow helps this type layer to stand out against the background image.

Tip

In the Layers panel, double-click anywhere in the layer effects list (or the fx icon if the layer effects list is closed) to reopen the Layer Style dialog box.

#49 Creating a Clipping Mask

If you've ever seen a picture in which text or a geometric shape is filled with photographic imagery, you've probably seen a *clipping mask* in action. A clipping mask is a stack of two or more layers in which the nontransparent content of the bottommost (or *base*) layer clips the content of the layers above it like a cookie cutter. A clipping mask can contain many layers, but they all have to be adjacent in the stack.

To create a clipping mask, do one of the following:

- If your clipping mask contains only two layers, press Alt (Windows) Option (Mac), and then position the cursor over the top edge of the base layer in the Layers panel (**Figure 49a**); two overlapping circles appear [icon]. When you see the overlapping circle icon, click.

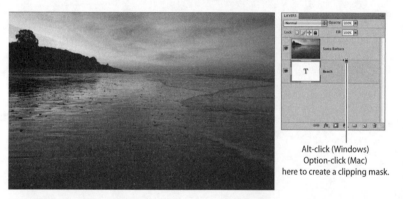

Alt-click (Windows)
Option-click (Mac)
here to create a clipping mask.

Figure 49a A two-layer image in which the top layer is a photograph and the bottom layer contains type.

- If your clipping mask contains more than two layers, in the Layers panel, select the layer(s) you want to include in the clipping mask (do not select the base layer), and choose Layer > Create Clipping Mask.

No matter which method you use, the name of the base layer will be underlined, and the rest of the layers in the clipping mask will be indented and marked with a right-angle arrow pointing down (**Figure 49b**).

Adding to a Clipping Mask

If you create a new layer between layers in a clipping mask or drag an unclipped layer between layers in a clipping mask, the layer becomes part of the clipping mask.

Clipping Mask Speed Tip

Speed up your work by learning this shortcut: To quickly create or release a clipping mask, select the layers you want to include in the mask and press Ctrl + Alt + G (Windows) Command + Option + G (Mac).

Clipping Mask icon

Clipping mask
Layer style effects

Figure 49b The beach layer now clips the Santa Barbara layer, and photographic imagery from the latter fills the word *beach*. In addition, two layer style effects were added to further enhance the effect.

Note
Layers in the clipping mask acquire the opacity and blending mode of the base layer.

CHAPTER SIX

Making Selections

One of my great privileges in life is having the opportunity to teach Photoshop at the Brooks Institute of Photography. From the get-go, the students are typically eager about learning how to make image modifications, adjustments, and corrections. My job is to redirect this enthusiasm and get them to realize that what they should be most interested in is learning how to make good selections. When working in Photoshop, you must select elements in the image before you can correct them. The quality of the selection often directly equates with the quality of the final adjustment.

A selection isolates one or more parts of an image. Making a selection allows you to edit and apply effects and adjustments to a specific part of your image. For example, when retouching a portrait, it is common to add a bit of sparkle to the eyes. To accomplish this effect, you select the eyes and then sharpen them. In this way, the eyes can be sharpened separately from the rest of the image.

You can make selections in Photoshop in numerous ways. This chapter discusses Photoshop's main selection tools, how to modify and customize selections, and how to make selections based on color. As you read through it, keep in mind that no single selection technique is best. Rather, the best technique is contingent upon the task at hand.

#50 Selecting with the Marquee Tools

The marquee tools let you select rectangles, ellipses, and single-pixel rows and columns. To begin using one of the marquee tools, select the tool in the Toolbox. Four tools share a single icon space; normally, only one is visible with three more hidden behind it. To access the hidden tools, click and hold on the visible marquee tool until the hidden tools appear (**Figure 50a**).

Figure 50a In the Toolbox, tool icons that are marked with a small triangle in the bottom-right corner conceal more tools that can be accessed by clicking and holding on the icon.

Choose the appropriate marquee tool to make a selection:

- **Rectangular Marquee.** Makes rectangular selections.

- **Elliptical Marquee.** Makes an elliptical selection.

- **Single Row or Single Column Marquee.** Selects columns a single pixel wide or rows a single pixel high.

Once a tool is selected, make a selection by dragging in the image. A selection is marked by small dashes that move around the selected area. In Photoshop circles, these are called "marching ants." To show or hide the marching ants, press Ctrl + H (Windows) Command + H (Mac) (**Figure 50b**).

Figure 50b Marching ants surround the three lights that have been selected in this image; each of which has been selected with the Elliptical Marquee tool.

Repositioning Marquee Selections

When making marquee selections, it can be difficult to place the selection in the correct position. Follow these steps to reposition selections:

1. Create the selection.

2. Continue to hold down the mouse button.

3. Press and hold down the spacebar and drag the selection to the desired position.

When you choose a marquee tool, options specific to the tool appear in the options bar. (The general options for the various selection tools will be discussed later in this chapter.) For the Rectangular and Elliptical Marquee tools, you can choose how the relationship between the height and width of the area you select is constrained. The choices are on the Style menu (**Figure 50c**):

- **Normal.** No constraint.

- **Fixed Ratio.** Constrains the selection to a fixed ratio between width and height, but the size is variable.

- **Fixed Size.** Constrains the selection to a size you choose. The size can be measured in pixels (px), inches (in), or centimeters (cm).

Practice Constraint

When dragging with either the Rectangular or Elliptical Marquee tool, holding down the Shift key constrains the selected area so that its height and width are equal. In other words, holding down Shift while using the Rectangular Marquee tool gives you a square selection, and doing the same while using the Elliptical Marquee tool gives you a perfectly round one.

One more keyboard tip that will help you position your selection more precisely: Holding down the Alt (Windows) Option (Mac) key while dragging centers the selection on the spot where you started dragging.

Figure 50c The Rectangular Marquee tool options as displayed in the options bar.

Tip
The Single Row or Single Column Marquee tools are useful for making a 1-pixel-wide selection or line. To make a 1-pixel-wide selection, select either tool, and then drag. To convert the selection to a line, choose Edit > Fill.

Tip
To quickly select the Marquee tool, press the M key. Next, press Shift + M to toggle through the other marquee tools.

#51 Using the Lasso Tools

Yeehaaa! In the Wild West, cowboys used lassos to catch and corral cows. In Photoshop, the lasso tools are used to make freeform, polygonal (straight-edged), and magnetic (snap-to) selections. For both the cowboy and the Photoshop user, the lasso can be a bit tricky. Once you get the hang of it, however, you'll find yourself reaching for the rope quite often.

To use the Lasso tool, select it in the Toolbox, or press and hold on the tool to view the three hidden lasso tools; each of which performs a different function (**Figure 51a**).

Figure 51a Select one of the three lasso tools in the Toolbox.

The Lasso tool is useful for making freeform selections. The Polygonal Lasso tool is useful for making selections that consist of a series of straight lines (but that can't be made by the Rectangular Marquee tool). And the Magnetic Lasso tool is useful for making quick selections of objects outlined by strong edges set against high-contrast backgrounds.

To use the Lasso tool, simply drag with it around the area you want to select. Then return to your starting point to close the loop.

To use the Polygonal Lasso tool:

1. Click on the image to set the first point.

2. Reposition the cursor and click again. This will create a straight line between the two points.

3. Continue creating straight lines and loop back to the first point (**Figure 51b**).

Fine-tuning: The Magnetic Lasso Tool Options

Setting the appropriate options for the Magnetic Lasso tool will help you create the best selection:

- **Width.** Enter a pixel value in the Width field so that the Magnetic Lasso tool only detects edges within the specified distance from the pointer.

- **Contrast.** The edge sensitivity is controlled by contrast. A low percentage detects low-contrast edges. A high percentage detects high-contrast edges.

- **Frequency.** To specify the rate at which the lasso sets anchor points, enter a value between 0 and 100 in the Frequency field. With a higher value, the selection border conforms to the edge you're trying to follow more quickly.

- **Stylus Pressure.** If you have a stylus tablet, select this option to use stylus pressure to adjust the edge width. For example, an increase in stylus pressure decreases the edge width.

Closing the Selection Border

To close the selection border, you have a couple of options:

- To close a border created by any of the three tools, drag back over the starting point and click.

- To close the border with a straight segment, hold down Alt (Windows) Option (Mac) and double-click.

- To close the border with a freehand Magnetic segment, double-click, or press Enter (Windows) Return (Mac) (Magnetic Lasso tool only).

Figure 51b In this image, I am using the Polygonal Lasso tool to select the "First Aid" graphics.

4. Click the first point to complete the selection.

The Magnetic Lasso tool is the most complex of the lasso tools. To use this tool:

1. Click to set the first anchor point.

2. Move the cursor along the edge you want to select (**Figure 51c**). The tool will automatically attempt to snap to the edge and create anchor points.

Figure 51c In this example, I have moved the Magnetic Lasso tool along the edge of the shadow to begin to make a selection of the shadow.

3. Continue moving the cursor along the edge and complete the selection by looping back and clicking on the first anchor point.

Tip
To make sure the Magnetic Lasso selects the correct edge, you can increase or decrease the width detection value while using the tool. To do this, press the right bracket] to increase the Magnetic Lasso edge width by 1 pixel; press the left bracket [to decrease the width by 1 pixel.

#52 Using the Quick Selection and Magic Wand Tools

The Quick Selection and Magic Wand tools make selections based on image characteristics. The advantage of using these tools is that you don't have to create or trace outlines. Rather, you set options, make a selection, and the tool does the rest.

Although what each of these tools accomplishes is similar, they go about it in different ways. The Quick Selection tool, as the name implies, lets you *quickly* "paint" a selection using an adjustable round brush tip. The tool is brilliant in that when you paint, it analyzes the surrounding pixels and grows the selection to include similar pixels (within clearly defined edges). The Magic Wand tool selects similar pixels based on color.

To use either tool, select it in the Toolbox (**Figure 52a**).

Figure 52a The Quick Selection and Magic Wand tools share a single icon in the Toolbox.

To use the Quick Selection tool, choose it and modify the options in the options bar (**Figure 52b**).

Quick Selection Modification

- To enlarge a selection once you have stopped clicking, click the Add To Selection button in the options bar and paint in another area. The selection will grow to include this new area.

- To subtract from a selection, click the Subtract From Selection button, and then drag over the area you want to deselect.

Figure 52b The options bar when the Quick Selection tool is active.

The options include the following:

- **Brush Size.** Choose the diameter of your brush (in pixels). Use a small brush size for smaller detailed selections, and a larger brush size for broader selections.

- **Sample All Layers.** Bases the selection on information from all layers instead of just the currently selected layer.

- **Auto-Enhance.** Automatically refines the selection edges. Leave this deselected if you want to have more manual control of the edge and intend to refine the edge by hand.

After you have chosen your options, paint inside the area of the image that you want to select. As you paint, the selection will automatically extend to the edge of the image area. Marching ants will surround the selected area.

To use the Magic Wand tool, select it and specify the options in the options bar (**Figure 52c**).

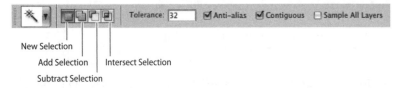

Figure 52c For more control, specify Magic Wand options in the options bar.

The options include the following:

- **Tolerance.** Defines the range of color that will be included in the selection. A low tolerance means that only pixels whose colors are very close to those clicked by the tool will be selected. A high tolerance value means that pixels with a broader range of colors will be included.

- **Anti-alias.** Creates a smoother-edged selection.

- **Contiguous.** Creates a selection only with adjacent areas that use the same colors. If the option is deselected, all pixels in the entire image using the same colors are selected.

- **Sample All Layers.** Makes a selection based on all layers, not just the current layer.

After you have specified the options, click the area you want to select. The selected area will be surrounded by marching ants.

A Tip on Brush Tips

When creating a selection, press the right bracket] to increase the diameter of your Quick Selection brush tip; press the left bracket [to decrease it.

#53 Modifying Selections

Many of the selections that you make will need to be modified, and each selection tool is equipped with different options to enable this. The options bars for the marquee tools, lasso tools, and the Magic Wand tool have a set of four buttons in common: New, Add To, Subtract From, and Intersect With. When the New button is selected, every time you click with the mouse, a new selection is created, and any current selection is lost. If the Add To or Subtract From button is selected, each click of the mouse adds to, or subtracts from, the current selection. When the Intersect With button is selected, new selections are retained only where they overlap previously selected pixels (**Figure 53**).

Figure 53 Options bar selection options.

Tip
Use these shortcut keys to quickly add or subtract from a selection. While a selection is active, press Shift to add or press Alt (Windows) Option (Mac) to subtract.

Another way to modify a selection is to use the Anti-alias option, which is available for the lasso tools, the Elliptical Marquee tool, and the Magic Wand tool in the options bar. Anti-aliasing is the process of filling in the gaps between the square pixels (by mixing together some of the color from outside the selection with the selected area) to create a smoother edge. This option is ideal for subtle, softer-edged selections. For harder-edged selections, you'll want to deselect anti-aliasing. Whatever choice you make, you'll need to select or deselect anti-aliasing before making a selection—you can't add it after the fact.

Tip
Anti-aliasing is useful when cutting, copying, and pasting selections to create composite images.

Feathering is available for the marquee and lasso tools. It works to blur edges of a selection by creating a transition area between the selection and its surrounding pixels by selecting some partial pixels. This blurring can cause some loss of detail at the edge of the selection. The loss of detail can be helpful when retouching or blending multiple images or adjustments.

To feather a selection, specify the amount of feathering in the options bar. Alternatively, you can choose Select > Modify > Feather, and then choose the amount.

The other commands on the Select menu can also be used to refine selections after you've made them:

- The **Expand and Contract** commands can be used with all types of selections. Choose Modify > Expand or Contract and specify a number between 1 and 100 pixels. This will uniformly increase or decrease the size of your selection based on the specified number, which comes in handy when you need to make small modifications.

- **Transform Selection** can be used with all kinds of selections. This allows you to reshape the geometry of the selection border by subjecting it to transform operations such as rotate, scale, or skew. If you are going to significantly increase or decrease the selected area, it is best to transform the selection (as opposed to using Expand/Contract). Choose Select > Transform Selection, and then drag one of the handles on the bounding box that surrounds the selection. The Transform Selection command also allows you to make free transformations.

- The **Grow and Similar** commands can be used with all selections. Both work to enlarge the selection; however, they accomplish this in different ways. Choose Select > Grow to enlarge the selection by adding contiguous pixels—in other words, those pixels surrounding the original selection. Choose Select > Similar to add pixels with similar color values from anywhere in the image. The Similar command uses the Tolerance setting in the Magic Wand tool. For more information, see #52.

Selection Speed Tip

To quickly modify selections, right-click (Windows) Control-click (Mac) the active selected area to open a context menu where you can choose from the following:

- Deselect
- Select Inverse
- Feather
- Refine Edge
- Save Selection
- Make Work Path
- Layer Via Copy
- Layer Via Cut
- New Layer
- Free Transform
- Transform Selection
- Fill
- Stroke
- Smart Sharpen
- Fade

Table 53 lists each selection tool and its different options.

Table 53 Selection Tool Options

Tool	Add To	Subtract From	Intersect	Antialias	Feather	Tolerance
Rectangular Marquee	√	√	√		√	
Elliptical Marquee	√	√	√	√	√	
Lassos	√	√	√	√	√	
Quick Selection	√	√	√			
Magic Wand	√	√	√	√		√

#54 Using the Refine Edge Tool

When you make a selection, you do not always know if the selection is a good one until you have applied an adjustment. If it isn't, you have to undo the adjustment and begin again. The Refine Edge tool takes selection precision to the next level. This tool lets you quickly view a selection against different backgrounds for fine-tuned editing.

To use the Refine Edge tool, first create a selection using one of the selection tools. Then click Refine Edge in the selection tool's options bar or choose Select > Refine Edge.

The Refine Edge dialog box opens (**Figure 54**).

Standard   On Black   Preview Mask

Quick Mask   On White

Figure 54 Modify the sliders to fine-tune the selection. Choose a preview mode to quickly identify problematic areas in the selection.

The sliders in this dialog box include the following:

- **Radius.** Defines the width of the zone around the selection boundary that will be affected by the Refine Edge dialog box. A higher radius creates a more exact selection boundary. Increase the radius to improve edges with soft transitions or fine detail.

- **Contrast.** Sharpens soft selection edges. Increase contrast to remove excessive noise near selection edges.

- **Smooth.** Smoothes irregular or jagged selection edges.

- **Feather.** Creates a uniform, soft-edged selection edge.

- **Contract/Expand.** Shrinks or expands a selection. Contracting (or shrinking) is particularly useful for removing unwanted fringes along the selection edge.

Use the preview mode buttons at the bottom of the dialog box to help identify problematic areas in the selection:

- **Standard.** View the selection as it normally appears.

- **Quick Mask.** View the selection with a transparent red overlay.

- **On Black/White.** View the selection against a black or white background.

- **Preview.** View the selection as a black-and-white mask.

#55 Selecting a Color Range

Using the Color Range command lets you make color-based selections. Color Range lets you target a specific color and dynamically adjust the reach of the selection to other colors.

To use the Color Range command:

1. Choose Select > Color Range to open the Color Range dialog box (**Figure 55a**).

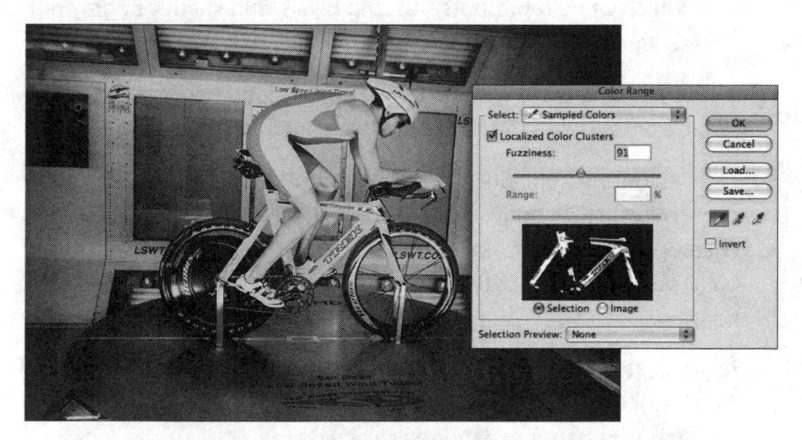

Figure 55a The Color Range dialog box. Because the yellow-colored bike had been sampled in the image using the Eyedropper tool, the bike shows up as white in the preview area in the dialog box.

2. Choose Sampled Colors from the Select menu (**Figure 55b**) and move the mouse pointer over the image, where it becomes an eyedropper.

Figure 55b The Select menu in the Color Range dialog box.

Pick a Color

You can also choose a specific color or tonal range from the Select menu in the Color Range dialog box. This method has a serious drawback, however: You can't adjust the selection, so its usefulness is limited.

Reset and Undo

In the Color Range dialog box (as well as in other places in the Photoshop interface), you can undo any adjustments you've made by resetting the values to their default values. To do this, press and hold down Alt (Windows) Option (Mac) to turn the Cancel button into a Reset button. Then click Reset.

3. Click an area in the image that has the color you want to select. All instances of that color in the image will be selected. The preview area in the center of the dialog box displays the selected area according to the options directly beneath the preview:

- **Selection.** Displays the selection depending on the option chosen from the Selection Preview menu. The default is a grayscale mask in which white represents selected pixels, and shades of gray represent partially selected pixels.

- **Image.** Reveals the entire image. This is helpful if you want to sample from a part of the image that isn't onscreen.

4. Select Localized Color Cluster to enable contiguous selections. This is a new option in CS4, but what does it actually do? Well as my friend Ben Willmore aptly says, "Color Range can be a bit greedy and Localized Color prevents this." In other words, this option prevents Color Range from "overselecting" colors from another area of the image.

5. To adjust the range of colors selected, use the Fuzziness slider on the left side of the dialog box. Drag the slider to the right to increase the color range and thus expand the selected area.

6. To add colors to the selection, choose the eyedropper icon with the plus (+) symbol and click additional colors in the image. To remove colors from the selection, choose the eyedropper icon with the minus (–) symbol, and then click in the image. Or press Shift-click to add and Alt-click (Windows) Option-click (Mac) to remove colors.

CHAPTER SEVEN

Using Blending Modes

I'll never forget the day when my artist Mom taught me about mixing paint—it was magic! I mixed some blue and yellow paint together, and all of a sudden I had created green! I was able to create something that was previously completely unimaginable. The same and more can be said about Photoshop's blending modes. They give you the ability to control not only how color blends together, but also how images, tone, type, and shapes blend. More specifically, blending modes enable you to control how the contents of one layer blend with the layer(s) below it.

You'll spend the first part of this chapter exploring how Photoshop blending works, and then you'll begin applying this knowledge to a number of scenarios. By the time you're finished reading and experimenting, you'll have a head start in using blending, which will catapult your creativity to previously unimaginable heights!

#56 Understanding Blending Modes

Photoshop has over two dozen blending modes, so the sheer quantity of options can be intimidating. Fortunately, because of the many similarities between blending modes, the options are not as complex as they first appear. Searching for the right blending mode is often a snap because the modes are grouped together based on their overall functionality, such as darkening, lightening, comparing, and color (**Figure 56a**).

Figure 56a While categorizing blending modes according to their functionality oversimplifies matters a bit, it will help you become familiar with how blending modes work.

When learning about the different blending modes and visualizing a blending mode's effect, it's helpful to be familiar with a couple of terms (**Figure 56b**):

- **Base color.** The original color in the image; the color of the bottom layer.

- **Blend color.** The color being applied; the color of the top layer.

Blend color

Base color

Figure 56b In this example, an image has been duplicated into a new layer, and the upper layer has been set to a blending mode. In scenarios such as this, the bottom layer can be referred to as the base color and the top layer as the blend color.

To get a handle on the specifics of blending modes, it's helpful to become familiar with the brief descriptions of the blending modes that follow.

Normal or Dissolve

- **Normal.** Default mode without blending.

- **Dissolve.** Blends with a random replacement of the pixels.

Darken

- **Darken.** Selects the base or blend color—whichever is darker—as the resulting color.

- **Multiply.** Multiplies the base color by the blend color. Black always produces black, and whites are unchanged.

- **Color Burn.** Uses the blend color to darken by increasing the contrast. Blending with white produces no change.

(continued on next page)

- **Linear Burn.** Darkens the base color to reflect the blend color by decreasing the brightness. Blending with white produces no change.

- **Darker Color.** Darkens based on all channels; only the lighter pixels on the blend layer remain.

Lighten

- **Lighten.** Similar to Darken, Lighten selects the base or blend color—except that it selects whichever is lighter—as the resulting color.

- **Screen.** Lightens in a similar way to projecting multiple photographic slides on top of each other.

- **Color Dodge.** Brightens the base color to reflect the blend color by decreasing the contrast. Blending with black produces no change.

- **Linear Dodge (Add).** Lightens the base color to reflect the blend color by increasing the brightness. Blending with black produces no change.

- **Lighter Color.** Lightens based on all channels; only the lighter pixels on the blend layer remain.

Contrast

- **Overlay.** Multiplies or screens the colors, depending on the base color. Blending with 50% gray has no effect.

- **Soft Light.** Darkens or lightens the colors, depending on the blend color. Blending with 50% gray has no effect.

- **Hard Light.** Multiplies or screens the colors, depending on the base color. Hard Light works like Overlay, but the blending is more intense. Blending with 50% gray has no effect.

- **Vivid Light.** Color dodges or burns, depending on the blend color. Blending with 50% gray has no effect.

- **Linear Light.** Color dodges or burns the colors by decreasing or increasing the brightness, depending on the blend color. Blending with 50% gray has no effect.

- **Pin Light.** Uses the Lighten blending mode for lighter colors and the Darken Blending mode for darker colors. Blending with 50% gray has no effect.

- **Hard Mix.** Creates a posterized image composed of up to eight colors: red, green, blue, cyan, magenta, yellow, black, and white. The blended color is a result of the base color and luminosity of the blend layer.

Comparative

- **Difference.** Subtracts either the blend color from the base color or the base color from the blend color, depending on which has the greater brightness value. This mode is useful for creative effects and determining the alignment of similar layers.

- **Exclusion.** Similar to Difference mode but a bit more muted and with less contrast. Blending with white inverts the base color values. Blending with black produces no change.

HSL

- **Hue.** Creates a resulting color with the luminance and saturation of the base color and the hue of the blend color.

- **Saturation.** Creates a resulting color with the luminance and hue of the base color and the saturation of the blend color.

- **Color.** Combines the luminance of the base color and the hue and saturation of the blend color. This mode is incredibly useful for coloring monochrome images and for tinting color images because the color is mapped to the grayscale tone of the image. So in effect you can see through the color to the image details.

- **Luminosity.** The blend layer is blended with luminance and does not affect the base color. This mode creates the opposite effect of Color blending mode.

Fade Command Conditions

The Fade command works only if invoked immediately after using a filter, painting tool, or color adjustment.

Scroll Through the Blending Modes

Sometimes you will know exactly which blending mode will work best. Other times, it is helpful to try different modes. The best way to do this is to scroll through the different modes:

1. Select the layer to be blended (the blend layer).

2. Select the Move tool (or press V).

3. Press Shift and the plus key (+) to scroll down or the minus key (-) to scroll up through the layer blending modes.

#57 Working with Blending Modes

Even though you may be able to access a particular blending mode in any of several areas of Photoshop—whether it's through the Layers panel, using the Fade, Fill, or Stroke commands, or any of the layer styles—it works the same regardless of how you access it. The trick is to learn where to find which blending mode in the different areas of Photoshop. Let's take a look at a few examples.

Blending via the Layers panel

The most common way to apply a blending mode is from the Layers panel:

1. Select a layer on the Layers panel.

2. From the Blend Mode menu at the top of the Layers panel, choose a blending mode (**Figure 57a**).

Figure 57a Here I wanted to blend the top layer into the underlying layers. I selected the top layer, "tape_corners." Then I chose the Soft Light blending mode, which blends the tape graphics into the underlying layers.

Blending via the Fade command

The Fade command can be used to change the opacity or blending mode of a filter operation, painting-tool application, or color adjustment after the fact.

For example, if you used the Brush tool to paint on your image and you wanted to modify that brush stroke, before you do anything else you would choose Edit > Fade or press Shift + Ctrl + F (Windows) Shift + Command + F (Mac), drag the Opacity slider, and/or choose a blending mode from the Mode menu (**Figure 57b**).

Figure 57b In the Fade dialog box, adjust the opacity, or choose a blending mode, or both.

Blending via the Brush tool

When using the Brush tool, you can choose a blending mode from the options bar. If you wanted to modify the color of someone's eyes, for example, you could do the following:

1. Choose the Brush tool and choose a color in the Color Picker.

2. In the options bar, choose Color from the Mode menu (**Figure 57c**).

Color blending mode

Figure 57c With the Brush tool active, choose a blending mode from the Mode menu in the options bar.

3. Paint with the brush directly on the eyes.

Because the Color blending mode is selected, painting with the brush changes the color of the eyes but leaves the luminance (the grayscale texture information) intact. The end result is an eye color that looks realistic. In contrast, painting with the brush without using the Color blending mode would result in a color brush stroke on top of (and not blended into) the image.

Blending Mode Shortcuts

Most of the time, selecting blending modes from a menu suffices. But if you want to take your skills to the next level, it's a good idea to learn the following shortcuts for selecting some çof the more common blending modes:

1. Select a layer.

2. Choose the Move tool.

3. Press Shift + Alt (Windows) Shift + Option (Mac), and then press one of the following letters:

- N = Normal
- M = Multiply
- S = Screen
- F = Soft Light
- O = Overlay
- C = Color

#58 Using the Multiply Blending Mode

The Multiply blending mode is one of the most commonly used darkening modes. The effect is similar to viewing two photographic transparency slides laid on top of each other. In more technical terms, this mode darkens by multiplying the base color by the blend color. Black always produces black, and whites are unchanged. The end result is a darker image.

To understand how the Multiply blending mode works, follow these steps:

1. Choose the Move tool and drag two images into one Photoshop document. Each image will be on its own layer.

2. Select the image in the top layer and change the blending mode to Multiply.

In **Figure 58a**, the image with the streetlights and the bright sky has been dragged on top of the image of the dark wall and set to Multiply mode. The resulting image is darker than either of the original pictures. Note especially how the whiter tones in the sky image have less impact.

Original images   Both images combined using the Multiply blending mode

Figure 58a The two original images on the left are blended using the Multiply mode, producing the blending and darkening result on the right.

While the previous blending example didn't improve the appearance of the image, don't let this dissuade you from using this mode. The example was to simply illustrate how the mode works. Let's move on to one practical use for the Multiply blending mode to improve an image. You can use this mode to darken an overexposed area of an image to correct the exposure. Let's use **Figure 58b** as an example in which the exposure of the image on the left needs to be corrected.

Figure 58b The original image (left) is overexposed. The exposure on the final image (right) has been corrected.

1. Working in the Layers panel, select the Background layer. Choose Layer > Duplicate.

2. With the newly duplicated layer still selected, choose Multiply from the Blend Mode menu. The image darkens noticeably.

3. To limit the darkening to the overexposed area of the face and hair, add a layer mask to the upper layer. Choose Layer > Layer Mask > Hide All to create a black mask that conceals the darkening effect.

4. Choose the Brush tool.

5. Click the Foreground Color box in the Toolbox to open the Color Picker and choose white.

6. Back in the Layers panel, click the layer mask to select it.

7. Paint with white on the bright areas of the subject's face to allow the darkening effect to show through the layer mask.

The final result is an image with a more correct and darkened exposure on the face of the subject.

Removing a White Background

Removing an object from a white background can be quite a complex and time-intensive task. Before diving in, try using the Multiply blending mode to get a quick (and rough) preview of what the object on a white background would look like removed from the background.

For example, consider a two-layer document in which the Background layer contains an image of a picnic table and the top layer contains an image of an apple photographed on a white background. The goal is to remove the apple from the white background and place it on the table. To get a rough preview of how this might look, do the following:

1. Select the apple layer and choose the Multiply blending mode. This will remove the white area so that only the apple remains.

2. If the apple is too faint, duplicate the apple layer to increase its density.

Following these steps can help you determine whether it would be worthwhile to invest the time in using selections, masks, and so on to separate the apple from the background.

#59 Using the Screen Blending Mode

The Screen blending mode is one of the most commonly used of the lightening modes. Its effect is similar to projecting multiple photographic slides on top of each other and results in an overall lightening of an image (**Figure 59a**).

Original images   Both images combined using the Screen blending mode

Figure 59a The original images on the left are blended together on the right using the Screen blending mode.

In contrast to the Multiply blending mode, the Screen blending mode modifies mainly the brighter tones in an image. In **Figure 59b,** for example, I created a few grayscale gradients and placed them in a layer above a background, as shown in the original image (top). I then changed the layer containing the gray items to Screen mode. The result (bottom) is that the brighter tones become brighter, whereas the blacks seem to disappear.

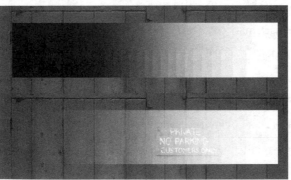

Original Grayscale

Grayscale blended with
Screen blending mode

Figure 59b The original gray gradient (top) is blended using the Screen mode (bottom).

One practical use of Screen mode is to brighten an underexposed area of an image. Here's how you might correct the exposure in **Figure 59c**:

Original image is underexposed and too dark

Corrected image is brighter and has a more correct exposure

Figure 59c The original image on the left is underexposed. The exposure was corrected by stacking a duplicate of the image set to Screen mode on top of the original. Then a layer mask was used to protect part of the image from the lightening effect.

1. Select the Background layer. Choose Layer > Duplicate.

2. In the Layers panel, choose Screen from the Blend Mode menu to brighten the overall image.

3. To limit the lightening to the underexposed area of the sky, add a layer mask to the upper layer. Choose Layer > Layer Mask > Reveal to create a white mask that reveals the brightening effect.

4. Choose the Brush tool.

5. Click the Foreground Color box in the Toolbox to open the Color Picker and choose black.

6. Back in the Layers panel, click the layer mask to select it.

7. Paint with black on the sky to remove the lightening effect.

The final result is an image with a more correct and appealing exposure.

#60 Using the Soft Light Blending Mode

As a photographer, you'll probably find that Soft Light is one of the blending modes you will use most often. This blending mode targets the darker and brighter tones but doesn't modify the middle grays. For this reason, there are many creative and practical photographic uses for Soft Light, such as combining multiple images, increasing contrast and color saturation, and burning and dodging (see #61). For example, **Figure 60a** illustrates how you can use blending to combine multiple images and add more contrast.

Original images   Both images combined using the Soft Light blending mode

Figure 60a The original images on the left are blended together on the right using the Soft Light blending mode.

To increase color saturation and contrast in an image using Soft Light mode, follow these steps:

1. Select the Background layer. Choose Layer > Duplicate.

2. With the new layer still selected, choose the Soft Light blending mode to increase the contrast and color saturation of the image (**Figure 60b**).

Figure 60b The final image (right) was created by duplicating the Background layer and changing the blending mode of the copy to Soft Light.

3. In the Layers panel, adjust the opacity of the Soft Light layer to achieve the effect you want.

#61 Burning and Dodging Using Blending Modes

Burning and dodging are photographic terms used to describe the technique of darkening or brightening tones in an image to create visual impact. Photoshop offers a number of different ways to burn and dodge; one of which is to use the Burn and Dodge tools in the Toolbox. However, the best approach is to use the Soft Light blending mode in combination with the Brush tool (**Figure 61**).

Figure 61 On the right, the corners of the image have been darkened or burned.

Using the Soft Light mode is useful because you can dodge and burn nondestructively. In other words, you will have the flexibility to undo or reduce the intensity of the dodging and burning. To effectively burn and dodge, follow these steps:

1. Select the Background layer. Choose Layer > New Layer.

2. With the duplicate layer still selected, choose the Soft Light blending mode.

3. Choose the Brush tool.

4. Press D to choose the default foreground and background colors, black and white, respectively.

5. Paint with black to darken (burn) or paint with white to brighten (dodge). (Press X to switch between black and white.)

In Figure 61, the original image (left) was modified using Soft Light and then painted with black to burn in details. To undo the burning effect, use a brush, select middle gray (#808080 in the Color Picker), and paint away the effect.

#62 Using Advanced Blending Techniques

In this chapter, you have thus far examined how to use blending modes as a way to blend entire layers. In most cases, these techniques will suffice. But there are times when you may need to blend only parts of layers together, perhaps only areas containing pixels within a certain tonal range. That is where the Advanced Blending feature comes into play.

For example, you can use Advanced Blending to make a selection of a subject's skin to soften the texture. To achieve this, follow these steps.

1. Open an image of a portrait.

2. Select the Background layer. Choose Layer > Duplicate Layer.

3. Click the Eye icon on the Background layer to hide the original Background layer.

4. Select the top layer, in other words, the new duplicate layer.

5. Click the *fx* icon at the bottom of the Layers panel and choose Blending Options from the menu. The Layer Style dialog box opens to the Blending Options: Custom pane (**Figure 62a**).

Figure 62a The Layer Style dialog box open to the Blending Options: Custom pane. The Advanced Blending controls occupy the bottom portion of the dialog box.

6. In the Advanced Blending area of the Layer Style dialog box, find the Blend If subarea. Drag the left This Layer slider to the right to remove (or blend) the dark tones.

7. Alt-drag (Windows) Option-drag (Mac) the left slider to split it into two smaller sliders.

8. Drag each triangle to create a smoother removal (or blending) of the dark tones. Click OK.

The final result (on the right) is a layer that contains only the brighter tones in the original image (**Figure 62b**).

Figure 62b In this example, Advanced Blending was used to select the brighter tones of the image. By blending away the darker tones, only the brighter skin tones remain.

9. Choose Filter > Blur > Surface Blur to soften the entirety of the Advanced Blending selection.

10. To limit the softening to the skin, choose the Eraser tool from the Toolbox. In the options bar, select a medium-size, soft-edged brush and 100% opacity. Erase any areas where the smoothing is not needed.

11. Click the Eye icon on the Background layer to make it visible again.

Note
Keep in mind that Advanced Blending is complicated, but it is well worth learning!

Tip
To quickly access the Advanced Blending controls, double-click on the layer to the right of the layer name.

Recovering Shadow Detail with Advanced Blending

Another common use of the Advanced Blending options is to recover shadow tones for printing. This is especially helpful when using the Soft Light blending mode (as described in #60). A negative side effect of using this blending mode is a darkening of the shadow detail to the extent that detail is lost.

If you follow the procedure in #60 and you find that you've lost some shadow detail, follow these steps:

1. Select the layer that has the Soft Light blending mode applied.

2. Open the Layer Style dialog box and switch to the Advanced Blending controls.

3. Move the left This Layer slider to the right. As you move the slider, watch the shadow detail and stop when you see an appropriate amount of it.

4. Alt-drag (Windows) Option-drag (Mac) the slider to split it into two sliders and adjust them to create a smooth transition.

#63 Creating a Blending Composite

One of the most powerful uses of blending modes is for creating composite images.

Creating an Expressive Composite

For the example in this how-to, I was interested in creating a visual piece that expressed my response to a poem. In particular, a line in the poem, which describes the slow passing of winter, struck me. With this thought in mind, I sought to create a visual that expressed my appreciation for the poem. To create your own expressive composite, look for things that inspire you.

No Rules

One of the nice things about creating a blending composite is that there are no rules, no limitations, and no such thing as common sense. As Picasso once said, "Common sense is the chief enemy of creativity." Having this type of attitude when it comes to creating blending composites can be incredibly freeing and lead you to new creative heights.

1. Open three images to be composited. In this example, from left to right you see a poem, a photograph of a leaf, and a photograph of a tree (**Figure 63a**).

Figure 63a Three elements before compositing.

2. Select the Move tool. Drag one or two of the images into the other image. Here the poem and tree were dragged into the leaf image. As you drag in the images, each one will be placed on a new layer.

3. Name the layers appropriately. In this example, appropriate choices would be poem, leaf, and tree.

4. Position the images to create an interesting composition.

5. Select the tree layer and choose the Soft Light blending mode.

6. Press Ctrl + I (Windows) Command + I (Mac) to invert the tree layer.

7. Select the poem layer. Click the Layer Style Effect icon in the Layers panel and choose Drop Shadow.

8. Click OK to apply the Drop Shadow effect.

Figure 63b The final result is a composite image that expresses a visual idea that could not have been communicated without blending.

CHAPTER EIGHT

Using Filters

In traditional photography, a filter is a glass element that you put on the front of the lens to affect the final image. In Photoshop, a filter works in a similar way in that it creates a new way to display the image. In contrast to traditional photography, with Photoshop you can apply and blend multiple filters in unique ways to deliver unlimited filtering possibilities.

Photoshop filters are used for a wide array of functions, from practical production tasks like sharpening to creative special effects like adding motion blur. Regardless of the task at hand, you use the same basic workflow steps to add and apply any kind of filter.

It's important to keep in mind that filters are multifaceted and can be applied in many different scenarios. To address them comprehensively would require many pages. This chapter focuses on only the essentials of filtering. However, as you're reading through it, try to get into the habit of continually envisioning other scenarios in which you might use a particular filter. When you have completed the chapter, take the time to experiment with the other filters: Experimenting is the best way to learn the many facets of each.

#64 Using Smart Filters

The Smart Filters feature gives you the ability to apply just about any Photoshop filter in a nondestructive manner. Exceptions include the Extract, Liquify, Pattern Maker, and Vanishing Point filters.

Nondestructive Smart Filters do not permanently modify pixels. Instead, when you apply a Smart Filter to an image, a set of "instructions" is recorded; when the image is displayed onscreen or output in some other manner, the output image is altered according to the instructions. The original pixel data, however, is preserved. You can modify, hide, or delete the instructions, and the filter effect is removed without affecting the original image.

To apply a Smart Filter, follow these steps:

1. Select a layer in the Layers panel.

2. Choose Filter > Convert for Smart Filters, and click OK in the dialog box that appears.

3. Apply a filter. For example, choose Filter > Noise > Add Noise.

4. Choose settings for the filter and click OK (**Figure 64a**).

Figure 64a Choose your settings in the filter dialog box.

When a layer has a Smart Filter applied, the filter appears below the layer in the Layers panel (**Figure 64b**). By default, the Smart Filter contains a mask filled with white that reveals the entire filter effect. To collapse or expand the list of Smart Filters, click the triangle at the right edge of the layer to which the Smart Filter is applied.

Figure 64b Smart Filters appear below the layer to which they are applied.

To restrict the effect of the filter to a portion of the image, paint with black on the filter mask (for more on masking, see Chapter 10, "Masking"). To edit the filter settings, double-click the name of the filter to reopen its dialog box.

You can also choose a blending mode for each Smart Filter:

1. Double-click the Edit Blending Options icon for the filter. The Blending Options (*filter name*) dialog box opens (**Figure 64c**).

2. Choose a blending mode from the Mode menu and/or change the Opacity setting.

Smart Speed Tip

Speed up your Smart Filter workflow with this short-cut: Rather than convert the layer to a Smart Object by way of the Filter pull-down menu, Ctrl-click (Windows) Command-click (Mac) on the layer, and then choose Convert to Smart Object from the context menu.

To Be or Not To Be . . . Smart

There are definite pros and cons to using Smart Filters.

On the positive side, Smart Filters are very flexible with built-in masks and controls to fine-tune the filter's strength and blending. Smart Filters also allow you to make nondestructive edits and adjustments. Having this "safety net" may help you to take more visual risks knowing that any adjustment can be reduced or completely removed.

At the same time, the flexibility and freedom of Smart Filters come at the price of file size and speed. Using Smart Filters can dramatically increase the size of your file and create longer save times depending on your particular computer configuration. So, while Smart Filters are designed to be flexible and save time, if you have an older computer, it may be best to reserve their use for situations when you feel the extra flexibility is helpful.

Figure 64c The Blending Options dialog box.

Note

To learn more about blending modes, see Chapter 7, "Using Blending Modes."

#65 Adding Blur

A plethora of techniques exists for adding blur in Photoshop. Rather than cover all these techniques, this chapter focuses on a few Photoshop blur filters that seek to replicate photographic blur: Gaussian Blur, Motion Blur, and Radial Blur.

Gaussian Blur

Gaussian Blur is useful for softening details in an image.

1. Select a layer in the Layers panel.

2. Choose Filter > Blur > Gaussian Blur to open the Gaussian Blur dialog box.

3. Drag the Radius slider to the right to increase the softening and blurring effect. The actual amount of the radius will depend on the image resolution. For low-resolution images like the one pictured in **Figure 65a**, try a low radius. For a high-resolution image, try a higher setting.

4. Click OK to apply the Gaussian Blur. Not surprisingly, the image becomes blurry.

Original   Final

Figure 65a Applying a Gaussian Blur with a Radius setting of 10 produced the image on the right.

Note
Too much Gaussian Blur can be overpowering. Try using Gaussian Blur with a low Radius setting to create a soft focus portrait, or make a selection and apply the blur to a specific area of an image.

Motion Blur

Traditional photographers create motion blur by taking a photograph of a moving object with an extended exposure time.

In Photoshop, the Motion Blur filter can be used to produce a similar blur effect. Here's how:

1. In the Layers panel, select the layer to which you want to apply motion blur.

2. Choose Filter > Blur > Motion Blur. The Motion Blur dialog box opens.

3. Specify a blur direction by entering a value in the Angle field (between –360° and +360°) and an intensity value in the Distance field (between 1 and 999). For this image, I have chosen a 21-degree angle and an intensity of 14.

4. Click OK to apply the Motion Blur filter (**Figure 65b**).

Figure 65b An image to which the Motion Blur filter has been applied.

Radial Blur: Spin

The Radial Blur filter using the Spin option simulates the soft blur created by a rotating camera.

1. Select a layer in the Layers panel.

2. Choose Filter > Blur > Radial Blur to open the Radial Blur dialog box.

3. Specify the amount and quality of the blur you want, and then select the Spin Blur Method. The actual amount setting will depend on the image resolution. For my image, I have set the amount to 17 and selected Good for the Quality setting.

4. Click OK. The filter applies a rotational blur to the image (**Figure 65c**).

Figure 65c The image with a Spin Radial Blur applied.

Radial Blur: Zoom

The Radial Blur filter with the Zoom option selected simulates the effect of a zooming camera to produce a soft blur.

1. Select a layer in the Layers panel.

2. Choose Filter > Blur > Radial Blur to open the Radial Blur dialog box.

3. Select the Zoom Blur method, choose an amount, and select a quality option. The actual amount will depend on the image resolution. In the example image in **Figure 65d**, I have chosen 17 for the amount and Good for the Quality setting.

4. Click OK. The filter applies a blur that mimics the effect of a camera zooming in on the image.

Figure 65d The image with a Zoom Radial Blur applied.

#66 Adding Film Grain

Recently, a friend of mine and editor of one of the world's major adventure sport magazines said, "Sometimes, digital is too perfect. I miss the texture, the personality, the grit, the life of film grain." Certain images can benefit from adding film grain, which sometimes adds more personality, dimension, depth, and nostalgia to an image. One way to reproduce the effect of film grain is to use the Film Grain filter, which applies an even pattern of noise to the image; a smoother pattern is used in the highlight areas.

1. In the Layers panel, select a layer.

2. Choose Filter > Artistic > Film Grain. The Filter Gallery opens with the Film Grain filter selected (**Figure 66a**).

Figure 66a The Filter Gallery.

3. Change the image preview zoom amount by clicking the plus (+) or minus (–) icons in the lower-left corner of the dialog box.

4. Adjust the Filter options by dragging these sliders:

   • **Grain** to increase or decrease the density of the grain.

   • **Highlight Area** to increase or decrease the percentage of the image treated as highlights.

   • **Intensity** to control the degree of the highlight brightening

(continued on next page)

Film Grain Plug-ins

Film grain can be added using Photoshop filters (as described in this how-to) or using third-party plug-ins, which need to be purchased separately. Two of my favorite film grain plug-ins are Exposure from Alien Skin (www.alienskin.com) and Color Efex Pro from Nik Software (www.niksoftware.com).

The actual slider values will depend on the image resolution. To create a more subtle effect, use lower values. In my example image, I have chosen Grain, 4; Highlight, 0; and Intensity, 1.

5. Click OK to apply the Film Grain filter.

After applying the Film Grain filter to a new layer, try using one of the blending modes on a duplicate layer (Chapter 7) or painting on the filter mask (Chapter 10) to limit the grain to specific areas. This will make the grain look more realistic. In **Figure 66b**, I duplicated the Background layer, added film grain, and then applied the Soft Light blending mode.

Original

With Film Grain added and Soft
Light blending mode applied

Figure 66b The bottom image shows the result of using the Film Grain filter on a duplicate layer and then applying the Soft Light blending mode.

#67 Using the Lens Correction Filter

In this chapter, so far, enhancement and effect filters have been covered. Now let's shift gears and examine a corrective filter.

The Lens Correction filter fixes common lens flaws, such as barrel and pincushion distortion, vignetting, and more. This filter is especially helpful with architectural photography, or in general when shooting with wide-angle lenses, or when shooting at a low position looking up (or a high position looking down). The results of this filter can be dramatic or subtle. Keep in mind that often it is the subtle improvements that differentiate a decent photograph from an amazing one.

For example, in **Figure 67a**, the Lens Correction filter was used to correct the image on the bottom. This is especially noticeable when you look at the black overlay lines I included to highlight the differences. Take note of the difference in the wood paneling on the left side and the back wall on the right in the before and after versions of the image.

Original

Distortion removed

Figure 67a The lower (and much more valuable) architectural image was corrected with the Lens Correction filter.

Lens Correction and Wide-angle Lenses

The following corrections are particularly helpful when shooting with extreme wide-angle lenses. You can make these corrections using the Lens Correction filter or in Adobe Camera Raw (Chapter 4, "Using Photoshop Camera Raw"). When possible, make them in Camera Raw, since it provides more accuracy and flexibility.

- **Chromatic Aberration** corrects color fringing. Zoom in on the image preview to get a closer view of the fringing as you make the correction.

- **Vignette** corrects images that have darkened edges. This can also be used for the creative purpose of intentionally darkening the corners to create a vignette.

- **Amount** sets the amount of lightening or darkening along the edges of an image.

- **Midpoint** specifies the width of area affected by the Amount slider. Specify a lower number to affect more of the image. Specify a higher number to restrict the effect to the edges of the image.

To apply the Lens Correction filter:

1. Select a layer in the Layers panel.

2. Choose Filter > Distort > Lens Correction. The Lens Correction dialog box opens (**Figure 67b**).

Figure 67b The Lens Correction dialog box.

3. Select Show Grid at the bottom of the dialog box.

4. Use the Size setting to adjust the grid spacing and the Color box to change the color of the grid.

5. Choose the Move Grid tool and drag the grid so that it aligns with the lines in the image. By comparing the grid with the lines in your image, you can determine how much correction is needed.

6. Adjust the Lens Correction sliders to correct the image. Here are the slider controls you will use most often:

   - **Remove Distortion** corrects two of the most common problems of lens distortion: barrel or pincushion distortion. Barrel distortion is a lens defect that causes straight lines to bow out toward the edges of the image (**Figure 67c**). Pincushion distortion is the opposite effect in which straight lines bend inward (**Figure 67d**). Drag the slider to the left to correct pincushion distortion or to the right to correct barrel distortion.

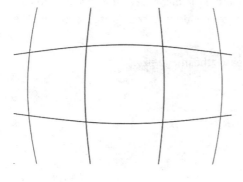

Figure 67c A grid showing barrel distortion.

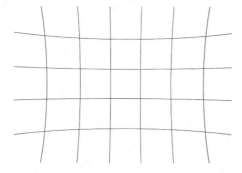

Figure 67d A grid showing pincushion distortion.

Tip
Choose or target the Remove Distortion control and drag on the image toward the center to correct for barrel distortion and toward the edge of the image to correct for pincushion distortion.

- **Vertical Perspective** corrects image perspective caused by tilting the camera up or down. This correction is especially helpful when shooting tall buildings from a low perspective. Drag the slider to make vertical lines in an image parallel.

(continued on next page)

Lens Correction and People

Distortion is easy to identify in the "straight and level" world of architectural photography. Thus, the Lens Correction filter is primarily used to correct distortions that occur in photography of structures, building, objects, and so on. At the same time, when used delicately, the Lens Correction filter can be a great asset when working on portraits. I have found that reducing lens barrel distortion on close-up head-shots is a particularly effective portrait enhancement.

- **Horizontal Perspective** corrects image perspective, making horizontal lines parallel.

- **Angle** rotates the image to correct for camera tilt.

- **Edge** specifies how to handle the blank areas that result from corrections. For the majority of situations, choose Transparency for the best results.

- **Scale** increases or decreases the image size.

7. Click OK to apply the filter.

CHAPTER NINE

Modifying Color and Tone

Color and tone evoke. Red can be fierce and full of passion. Yellow can be warm and nostalgic. Blue can be cold and isolating. Deep and dark tones can draw in the viewer. Flat and dull tones can stir up distant vague memories. Take the two forces of color and tone, mix them together, and you have the capability to create inexplicable visual impact. This chapter delves into the wonderful world of using Photoshop to modify color and tone.

While Photoshop's strengths are broad and deep—similar to an athlete who performs well in multiple sports—perhaps the arena where Photoshop excels most is in color and tone. No other digital imaging application comes close to rivaling the color and tone tools in Photoshop. This chapter shows you how to use essential tools like Levels, Curves, Hue/Saturation, Color Balance, Photo Filters, and more so that you can begin to make profound color and tone enhancements to your images.

Keep in mind, however, that because of the inherent wonders and complexities of color and tone, it can take a lifetime to learn how to approach them. The best artists often learn the essential skills and then approach color and tone as a mystery to be experienced rather than a problem to be solved. Just as Picasso once pondered, "Why do two colors, put one next to the other, sing? Can one really explain this?"

The techniques you learn in this chapter should provide a foundation from which to work as you explore the power of color and tone. They should also help you create images that connect more vividly with your viewers.

#68 Adjusting Levels

Almost all images need some fine-tuning using Levels or Curves, so let's begin by discussing Levels. You can use the Levels dialog box to correct the tonal range and color balance of an image by adjusting the intensity levels of image shadows, midtones, and highlights.

1. To adjust the key tones in an image, select the layer you want to work on, and then choose Image > Adjustments > Levels, or even better, navigate to the Adjustments panel and click the Levels icon to create a Levels adjustment layer (**Figure 68a**).

2. In the Adjustments panel, select Shadows, Midtones, or Highlights to select the tonal range in which you want to modify.

Histogram   Histogram   Apply auto color correction

Channel menu

Shadows slider

Highlights slider

Midtones slider

Figure 68a Think of the Levels dialog box as a way to visually adjust color and tone.

3. Move the Shadows, Midtones, or Highlights sliders to make adjustments. Think of the Levels dialog box as a visual guide for controlling and correcting exposure:

- If an image is overexposed, move the Shadows slider to the right to increase the darker tones.

- If an image is underexposed, move the Highlights slider to the left to decrease the brighter tones.

- To control the overall brightness of an image, move the Midtones slider to the left to lighten it or to the right to darken it. It may be helpful to think of the Midtones slider as a dimmer switch. While it doesn't turn the lights on or off, it does control the overall brightness.

One of the most common reasons to use Levels is to fix images that are "flat" and lack tonal variety and contrast. For example, **Figure 68b** is a washed-out image with limited contrast. It was much improved by opening the Levels dialog box and dragging the Shadows slider to the right to increase the darker tones and then dragging the Highlights slider to the left to decrease the brighter tones. This produced an enhanced image (**Figure 68c**).

Figure 68b The original image before any adjustments.

What Is a Histogram?

You may remember the discussion of histograms in Chapter 2, "Working with Digital Image Files," where you glanced briefly at the histogram in the Levels dialog box. Histograms are found on certain high-end cameras and in various other places in Photoshop, such as in the Curves dialog box, the Camera Raw dialog box, the Histogram panel, and so on. Here's a quick refresher on the histogram and its importance:

- A histogram illustrates how pixels in an image are distributed by graphing the number of pixels at each brightness level.

- Histogram information is helpful because it reveals whether the image contains enough detail in the shadows, midtones, and highlights.

- Histogram information can be used to correct exposure and color.

Figure 68c In the Levels dialog box, the Shadows slider was dragged to the right and the Highlights slider was dragged to the left to create a more natural tonal range in the image.

Note

*At the bottom of the Adjustments panel, you will find a series of helpful icons that are visible with every type of adjustment (**Figure 68d**).*

Figure 68d The icons at the base of the Adjustments panel can be selected for all types of adjustments.

#69 Using the Curves Dialog Box

Both the Curves and Levels dialog boxes can be used to adjust the entire tonal range of an image. However, the difference between the two boils down to precision. Whereas the Levels dialog box contains three sliders for making adjustments, the Curves dialog box lets you adjust up to 14 different points throughout an image's tonal range (from shadows to highlights). As one of my fellow teachers often says, "Curves is Levels on steroids."

To apply a Curves adjustment, select the layer you want to work on. Choose Image > Adjustments > Curves, or even better, navigate to the Adjustments panel and click the Curves icon 🔲 to create a Curves adjustment layer (**Figure 69a**). From here you can make your adjustments.

Using Image > Adjustments > Curves

When you choose Image > Adjustments > Curves, keep in mind that this method makes direct adjustments to the image layer and is therefore much more limiting.

Figure 69a Curves lets you make precision adjustments to the color and tone of an image.

At first glance, the Curves dialog box can be intimidating. But once you begin, you'll find that applying an adjustment is easier than you thought it would be. I tend to apply a Curves adjustment to almost all of my images.

If making Curves adjustments are new to you, try starting off using the On-image adjustment tool (Figure 69a). This tool is new to CS4, and it allows you to quickly make adjustments to specific areas of your image.

Advanced Color with Curves

One of the most powerful aspects of Curves is that it gives you the ability to make precise adjustments to the different color channels of your image:

1. In the Curves dialog box, choose an individual color channel from the Channel menu. If you are working on an RGB image, for example, choose one of the following:

   - Red to modify: Red and Cyan
   - Green to modify: Green and Magenta
   - Blue to modify: Blue and Yellow

2. Once you have chosen a specific channel, click the Curve line and drag it up to lighten that channel's color and down to lighten the channel's complementary color. For example, in the Red channel, drag up to add red. Drag down to add cyan.

Click the tool icon, and then position the cursor over the area of the image you want to modify. Next, click-drag up to increase or click-drag down to decrease the values of that area. Once you've tried this tool, you'll discover that it will help you make visual evaluations and both subtle and strong improvements to your images.

On the other hand, you can move the curve line. For example, one of the most commonly applied and classic Curves adjustments is the *S* curve. In the Curves dialog box, the shape of the curve can be modified to change the color saturation, contrast, and tone of your image.

To apply an *S* curve:

1. In the Curves dialog box, do any of the following:

   - Click the curve line near the top (near the Highlights endpoint) and drag up to lighten the highlights.

   - Click the curve line near the bottom (near the Shadows endpoint) and drag down to darken the shadows.

   - Click the curve line near the middle (in the Midtones area) and drag up or down to adjust the overall brightness.

Figure 69b shows an image in desperate need of an *S* curve because the image lacks contrast and color saturation.

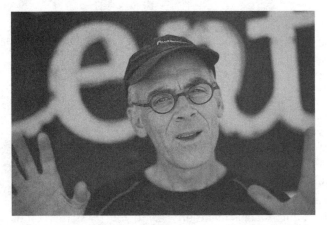

Figure 69b This image needs a Curves adjustment to increase contrast and color saturation.

Figure 69c shows how the curve was adjusted in an effort to fix the image.

Figure 69c Darkening the shadows and brightening the highlights produced the classic *S* curve.

2. Click OK to apply the adjustment and view the final result.

Figure 69d shows the result of applying an *S* curve adjustment to Figure 69b.

Figure 69d The final image as a result of the *S* curve adjustment.

Curves Shortcut

If you make a lot of Curves adjustments—and chances are you will—here's a shortcut you may find helpful: Select a layer in the Layers panel and press Ctrl + M (Windows) Command + M (Mac) to open the Curves dialog box.

Curves Precision

For more precise control of curves, press Alt (Windows) Option (Mac) while clicking anywhere inside the grid area to change a 4 × 4 grid to a 10 × 10 grid.

#70 Adjusting Hue and Saturation

The Hue/Saturation command lets you adjust the hue (color), saturation (color intensity), and brightness of an image. These controls are of equal value to both technical and creative image makers.

To apply a Hue/Saturation adjustment:

1. Click the desired layer and choose Image > Adjustments > Hue/ Saturation, press Ctrl + U (Windows) Command + U (Mac), or even bet- ter, navigate to the Adjustments panel and click the Hue/Saturation icon ▰ to create a Hue/Saturation adjustment layer (Figure 70).

Figure 70 The Hue/Saturation dialog box provides controls to modify color, saturation, and brightness.

2. Do any of the following:

   - Drag the Hue slider to shift all the colors in the image around the color wheel. As you drag, the colors in the Modified Color bar at the bottom of the dialog box move in relation to the Original Color bar.

   - Move the Saturation slider to the right to increase saturation or to the left to decrease or remove saturation.

   - Move the Lightness slider to the right to increase lightness or to the left to decrease lightness.

   - Select the On-image adjustment tool. Position the cursor over the image and click-drag to the left to decrease or to the right to increase the Saturation amount of the color that you clicked on.

Using Image > Adjustments > Hue/ Saturation

When you choose Image > Adjustments > Hue/ Saturation, keep in mind that this method makes direct adjustments to the image layer and is therefore much more limiting.

Advanced Hue/ Saturation Technique

By default, the Master channel is selected in the Edit menu of the Hue/ Saturation dialog box. This default setting is great when making global adjustments. However, for more precise control, you can choose a specific color from the menu to adjust only that color. For example, in a recent pho- tograph I shot of a woman in a red dress, the dress was overexposed. To adjust only the color of the dress, I chose the Red channel and then decreased the Saturation and Lightness sliders by 5 points. This corrected the exposure of only the reds in the image, but left the rest of the colors intact.

#71 Adjusting Color Balance

If you are a visually oriented person, you will really like the Color Balance command because it is both intuitive and visually easy to understand. In more particular terms, Color Balance changes the overall colors in an image. If you are looking for a tool to make strong global color adjustments, Color Balance is your tool.

To apply a Color Balance adjustment:

1. Select the desired layer and choose Image > Adjustments > Color Balance, press Ctrl + B (Windows) Command + B (Mac), or even better, navigate to the Adjustments panel and click the Color Balance icon to create a Color Balance adjustment layer (**Figure 71**).

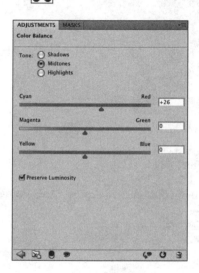

Figure 71 Use the Color Balance dialog box to make general color corrections and modifications to the shadows, midtones, and highlights in your image.

2. To maintain a tonal balance in the image, leave the Preserve Luminosity option selected to prevent changing the luminosity values in the image while changing the color.

3. Select the Shadows, Midtones, or Highlights radio button to indicate the tonal range where you want to focus the changes.

4. Drag each slider toward a color that you want to strengthen in the image and away from a color that you want to weaken in the image.

Color Balance

When you choose Image > Adjustments > Color Balance, keep in mind that this method makes direct adjustments to the image layer and is therefore much more limiting.

Color Balance, Sunsets, and Sepia Tones

The Color Balance command can be used for a wide array of color modifications. To learn more about how this tool works, try using the command on a photograph of a sunset. You will be amazed at the results!

1. Open the Color Balance dialog box and increase the Red by 40 points.

2. Modify Yellow or Blue, depending on the image. Try adding 40 points to one or the other.

Similarly, to apply a sepia tone to a black and white image, use this same technique. But instead increase Red by 30 points and reduce Yellow by 30 points.

#72 Replacing Color

The Color Replacement tool is a good choice when you need to replace the color of a specific object with another one, whereas the Replace Color command is a good choice when you need to make a global color change.

Using the Color Replacement tool

To use the Color Replacement tool:

1. Choose the Color Replacement tool from the Toolbox (it's hidden behind the Brush tool) (**Figure 72a**).

Figure 72a The Color Replacement tool shares a spot on the Toolbox with the Brush tool.

2. Configure the following settings in the options bar (**Figure 72b**):

Figure 72b The options bar for the Color Replacement tool.

- **Brush.** Modify the size of the brush to match the size of the color object you want to change.

- **Mode.** The Color setting typically works best.

- **Sampling.** To sample colors continuously as you drag, choose Continuous. To replace the targeted color only in areas containing the color that you first selected, choose Once. To replace only the areas containing the current background color, choose Background Swatch.

- **Limits.** To replace the sampled color wherever it occurs under the pointer, choose Discontiguous. To replace colors that are part of a continuous area, including the color immediately under the pointer, choose Contiguous. To replace connected areas containing the sampled color while better preserving the sharpness of shape edges, choose Find Edges.

- **Tolerance.** Choose a low percentage to replace colors very similar to the pixel you click, or raise the percentage to replace a broader range of colors.

- **Anti-alias.** Select this option to define a smooth edge in the corrected areas.

3. Paint in the image to replace the targeted color.

Using the Color Replace command

To use the Color Replace command:

1. Choose Image > Adjustments > Replace Color to open the Replace Color dialog box (**Figure 72c**).

Figure 72c The Replace Color command works effectively when you need to make global color replacements.

Why Replace Color?

The Color Replace command and the Color Replacement tool are very powerful features of Photoshop. However, many photographers often assume that color replacement is used only when creative and subjective edits are desired. While these features are useful for those types of applications, they are also helpful for printing images in which the color is out of gamut (the range of colors an output device is capable of producing). In these cases, you can use Replace Color or Color Replacement to replace an out-of-gamut color with a color that is in gamut. This gives you full control of the final output.

2. Select a display option by choosing either the Selection radio button, which displays the mask in the preview window, or the Image radio button, which displays the image in the preview window.

3. Use the Eyedropper tool and click the area of the image or the preview box where you want to replace the color. If you need to add areas of color, use the Add to Sample tool. If you need to subtract areas of color, use the Subtract from Sample tool.

4. Adjust the tolerance by dragging the Fuzziness slider to the right to increase the degree to which related colors are included in the selection.

5. Choose a replacement color by dragging the Hue, Saturation, and Lightness sliders. You can see a live preview of the color change in the preview window.

6. Click OK to apply the color replacement.

#73 Adjusting Shadows and Highlights

A broad range of brightness and shadows while photographing a scene can make it difficult to get the exposure correct. For example, in **Figure73a**, the background is properly exposed, but the boy is too dark. This commonly happens when the light source (in this case the sky) is behind a subject.

Figure 73a Here just the subject is underexposed.

To remedy such problems, you can use the Shadow/Highlight command (**Figure 73b**).

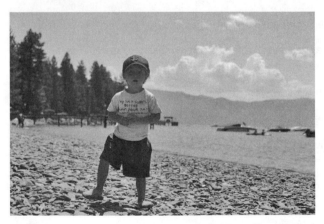

Figure 73b Using the Shadow/Highlight command improved the exposure and brightened the previously underexposed subject in this image.

Why Does Shadow/Highlight Work?

Unlike other controls in Photoshop CS4, the Shadow/Highlight command does not simply lighten or darken an image. Rather, it lightens or darkens a part of the image based on the surrounding pixels. And this is why Shadow/Highlight works so well. The analysis of the surrounding pixels results in better darkening and brightening. Separate controls for the shadows and the highlights, as well as a Midtone Contrast slider, Black Clip option, and White Clip option for adjusting the overall contrast of the image only add to the rich functionality of the Shadow/Highlight command.

The Shadow/Highlight command works well for correcting photos that contain silhouetted images that are the result of strong backlighting or for correcting subjects that have been slightly washed out because they were too close to the camera flash.

To use the Shadow/Highlight command:

1. Choose Image > Adjustments > Shadow/Highlight to open the Shadows/Highlights dialog box (**Figure 73c**).

Figure 73c The Shadows/Highlights dialog box.

2. Select the Show More Options check box to reveal more controls.

3. Adjust the Shadows sliders to brighten shadow details. Then adjust the Highlights sliders to darken highlight details.

For both the Shadows and Highlights areas:

- Use the Amount slider to control the intensity of the adjustment.

- Use the Tonal Width slider to control how much of the tonal range of the image will be affected.

- Use the Radius slider to control the pixel width of the corrected area.

4. Use the Color Correction and Midtone Contrast sliders to compensate for any undesirable color or contrast changes you notice as you're making your adjustments.

#74 Using Brightness and Contrast

In previous versions of Photoshop, the Brightness/Contrast command was not very effective unless it was used for special effects. However, the new and improved Brightness/Contrast command in CS4 works much better. It lets you make simple adjustments to the tonal range of an image. And because you can control both brightness and contrast separately, you can rectify the dark areas of an image that result from increasing the contrast by increasing the brightness, too.

To correct brightness and contrast:

1. Choose Image > Adjustments > Brightness/Contrast to open the Brightness/Contrast dialog box (**Figure 74a**). Or even better, navigate to the Adjustments panel and click the Brightness/Contrast icon to create a Brightness/Contrast adjustment layer.

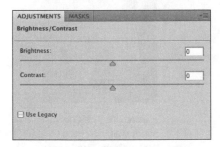

Figure 74a The Brightness/Contrast dialog box.

2. Move the sliders to the right to increase brightness or contrast and to the left to decrease brightness or contrast.

The most important setting in Brightness/Contrast is the Use Legacy option (which makes the command work the way it did in earlier versions of Photoshop).

In default mode, the option is not selected, so brightness and contrast adjustments are proportionate (nonlinear) to the image pixels. The way these adjustments are made is similar to the way Levels and Curves adjustments are made.

In contrast, when Use Legacy is selected, adjustments to brightness simply shift all pixel values higher or lower, which can cause clipping and loss of detail. This is a problem because while this loss of detail may look good on your monitor, it will most likely have a negative appearance when the image is printed. As a result, this option is helpful when creating special effects, but it's not ideal for high-end print output.

Figure 74b shows an image without adjustments. **Figures 74c** and **74d** illustrate the difference between the default and Use Legacy modes. Both images were adjusted using the Brightness/Contrast command in the same fashion: The contrast was increased to 100. However, Figure 74c was adjusted in default mode, whereas Figure 74d was adjusted with Use Legacy selected.

Figure 74b The original image without any adjustments.

Figure 74c The Contrast slider was increased to 100 with the Use Legacy option deselected.

Figure 74c The Contrast slider was increased to 100 with the Use Legacy option deselected.

#75 Applying Photo Filters

In traditional film photography, it is a common practice to put a colored filter in front of the camera lens to adjust the color balance and temperature. This gives photographers creative control over the color shift of an image. For example, for many years, a popular filter has been the 85 warming filter, which adds a yellow or warm tone and creates a nostalgic and inviting image. The Photo Filter command mimics this traditional photographic technique and gives digital photographers the same creative control.

To apply a photo filter:

1. Choose Image > Adjustments > Photo Filter to open the Photo Filter, or even better, navigate to the Adjustments panel and click the Photo Filter icon 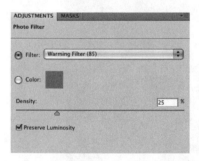 to create a Photo Filter adjustment layer (**Figure 75**).

Figure 75 Choose a preset filter to warm or cool the image. Or select a custom color to correct a color cast or for special color effects.

2. Do one of the following:

   • Select the Filter radio button and choose a preset filter from the Filter menu.

   • For a custom color filter, select the Color radio button, click the color square to the right, and use the Adobe Color Picker to specify a color.

3. Adjust the amount of color applied using the Density slider. A higher number results in a stronger color adjustment.

4. To prevent the image from being darkened by the color filter, select the Preserve Luminosity option.

5. Click OK to apply the filter to the image.

Preset Photo Filters

The Warming Filter presets make the image warmer (more yellow), and the Cooling Filter presets make the image cooler (bluer). Which filter is best? It depends on the desired intensity of the color effect:

• Warming Filter (81) and Cooling Filter (82) are best for minor adjustments.

• Warming Filter (85 and LBA) and Cooling Filter (80 and LBB) are best for making strong adjustments.

Another option is to select the Color radio button to apply a global hue adjustment to the image. A custom color can be used to neutralize a color cast or to apply colors for special color effects or enhancements. While it is possible to use the Color option for correcting color casts, I find it most helpful for special effects.

#76 Converting to Black and White

There is something powerful about a good black-and-white image. Fortunately, creating a compelling one is much easier than it used to be. The Black & White command in Photoshop CS4 allows you to convert a color image to grayscale while maintaining full control over how individual colors are converted. You can even tint the grayscale image with a color to create sepia or other tone effects.

It's also possible to use the Hue/Saturation command for black-and-white conversions, but it's less precise and thus works much less effectively than the Black & White command. For example, **Figure 76a** was converted to grayscale using the Hue/Saturation command, whereas **Figure 76b** was converted using the Black & White command.

Figure 76a A grayscale conversion using the Hue/Saturation command.

Figure 76b The same image converted to grayscale using the Black & White command.

To use the Black & White command:

1. Choose Image > Adjustments > Black & White, or even better, navigate to the Adjustments panel and click the Black and White icon ▨ to create a Black/White adjustment layer. When you open the dialog box, Photoshop performs a default grayscale conversion based on the colors in the image.

2. If you do not like the default conversion, click the Auto button. I have found that this creates a much more desirable starting point.

3. Manually adjust the conversion using the color sliders or choose a preset or previously saved custom mix from the Preset menu (**Figure 76c**).

Black and White Video Tutorial

Look for the free tutorial video on converting color images to black and white on http://tv.adobe.com.

A Black and White Speed Tip

You can use the cursor to make more precise black-and-white adjustments.

1. Open a color image.

2. Choose Image > Adjustments > Black & White.

3. With the Black and White dialog box open, hover the cursor over the image until the cursor changes to an eyedropper.

4. Click an area in the image, and the corresponding color will be selected in the dialog box. Without releasing the mouse button, drag to adjust the color slider for that color.

This technique is incredibly helpful because you don't have to guess which slider affects a particular area in the image. Instead, you simply hover over a color in the image, and then drag to make changes. Not only does this speed tip make

Figure 76c Choose one of the default black-and-white presets or choose a previously saved custom mix.

4. For any of the colors in the original image, drag the corresponding slider to the left to darken or to the right to lighten the gray tones of that color. For example, to darken the sky, drag the blue and cyan sliders to the left.

5. An alternative method is to use the On-image adjustment tool (Figure 76c). Click the tool icon, and then position the cursor over the area of the image you want to modify. Next, click-drag right to increase or click-drag left to decrease the luminance values of that area. Once you've tried this tool, you'll be hooked because it allows you to make compelling black-and-white conversions with ease.

6. To enhance your black-and-white image by adding a color tone, select the Tint option and adjust the Hue (color) and Saturation (color intensity) sliders. Or click on the color chip to the right of the Tint option to choose a tint color from the Adobe Color Picker. Note: The color chip only appears after you have selected Tint.

#77 Using the Dodge and Burn Tools

The Dodge and Burn tools can be used in combination to darken (burn) or brighten (dodge) different areas of your image. These tools go hand-in-hand because they belong together, just like peanut butter and jelly. In fact, you will rarely hear someone talk about one tool without the other.

Learning how to dodge and burn is a bit of an art form, but there is good news. In the previous versions of Photoshop, these tools were not half as useful. A new control called Protect Tones finally elevates these tools to the top of a photographer's regular workflow tools. To use the tools, follow these steps:

1. Select the Dodge tool or the Burn tool from the Tools panel (**Figure 77a**), and then determine the options in the options bar (**Figure 77b**).

Figure 77a The Dodge and Burn tools.

Figure 77b The menu options in the options bar for the Dodge and Burn tools are identical.

2. Choose a brush tip and set brush options in the options bar. Usually, it is best to choose a brush that is smaller than the area you are working on. In addition, typically soft-edged brushes work best.

Dodge and Burn Video

To learn more about how to use the Dodge and Burn tools, look for the free tutorial video on http://tv.adobe.com.

Traditional Photographic Dodging and Burning

Dodging and burning in Photoshop is based on traditional darkroom techniques that involved decreasing or increasing the exposure in specific areas of the print. The end result was the ability to brighten or darken the final print to create more compelling photography. In fact, it was Ansel Adams who really elevated dodging and burning to a new level. He wrote a revered book on the subject titled *The Print*. If you have never thumbed through or read Ansel's book, I highly recommend it. Even though you can dodge and burn digitally, I still think you might learn a thing or two.

3. In the options bar, select one of the following from the Range menu to target or limit the area that is affected:

- **Midtones.** Changes the middle range of grays
- **Shadows.** Changes the dark areas
- **Highlights.** Changes the light areas

4. Specify the low exposure amount for the Dodge tool or the Burn tool so you can slowly build up the effect.

5. New to CS4 is the ability to select the Protect Tones option to minimize clipping in the shadows and highlights. In other words, this option works to keep colors from shifting hue and in addition it makes your dodging and burning look much more natural (**Figure 77c**).

Image is too dark / Image brightening looks unnatural / The final results are much more natural and compelling

Original / Brightened with Dodge tool; Protect Tones off / Brightened with Dodge tool; Protect Tones on

Figure 77c The original image (left) is underexposed. The middle image was brightened using the Dodge tool with Protect Tones turned off. The image on the right was brightened using the Dodge tool with Protect Tones turned on, resulting in an image that looks more natural and has a more proper exposure.

6. Finally, click and drag over the part of the image you want to lighten or darken. Keep in mind that it is almost always best to start with a subtle effect that you slowly build up. Therefore, paint back and forth until you have reached the desired effect.

CHAPTER TEN

Masking

My older brother and I used to love running around wearing our favorite Spiderman, Batman, or Zorro masks when we were little. Masks are fun, especially for kids, because they hide a portion or all of your face. Photoshop layer masks work in a similar way in that they can be used to partially or entirely hide something, particularly the contents of a layer.

And here's the *really* good news. While masking isn't easy, it definitely isn't rocket science. Once you master the basics of masking, the efficiency of your Photoshop workflow will grow by leaps and bounds.

This chapter presents the fundamental concepts that will help you better understand and work with masks. As you read through it, keep the following in mind:

- Because masking is so important, slow down, absorb the information, and then make sure you practice each of the how-tos presented here. Don't just read along.

- While this chapter presents just the essentials of masking, you can apply the techniques to a wide range of simple and advanced image edits and enhancements.

- If you feel like masking is difficult, don't give up. Your efforts will pay off when you see the results!

#**78** Using a Layer Mask

One way to use a mask is to attach it to a specific layer. Masks can be added to any type of layer: image layers, adjustments layers, type layers, shape layers, layer groups, and so on. The advantage of using a layer mask is that when you add a mask to a layer and hide a portion of it, you are not actually deleting pixels; instead, you are simply hiding them. So if you make a mistake or change your mind, you can always go back and modify the mask.

To add a mask to a layer, select the layer and do one of the following:

- Click the Add a Layer Mask icon in the Layers panel (**Figure 78a**) or in the Masks panel (**Figure 78b**).

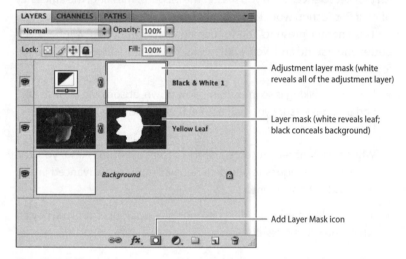

Figure 78a The quickest way to add a layer mask is to select the layer and click the Add Layer Mask button in the Layers panel. The mask will appear to the right of the layer thumbnail.

Figure 78b First click on the Masks tab to open the Masks panel, and then click the Add a Pixel Mask icon to add a mask. It will appear to the right of the layer.

- Choose Layer > Layer Mask > Reveal All or Hide All.

The key to understanding masks is that white reveals and black conceals. You can click on a mask to select it, and then paint on it using white or black to show or hide the contents of the layer.

For example, in **Figure 78c**, I want to select the leaf to remove it from its background. I used the selection tools to select everything but the leaf (in other words, the background) and then painted the selection black. The result is the leaf by itself (**Figure 78d**).

Figure 78c The original image.

Figure 78d The background was removed using a layer mask.

Keep in mind that no pixels were harmed using this technique. I can also return and modify or remove the mask at anytime by painting with black or white (see #79 for more information).

Use the Same Layer Mask on Multiple Layers

There are a number of circumstances in which you may need to apply identical or similar masks to multiple layers. The quickest way to apply a layer mask from one layer to another is to duplicate the mask by holding Alt (Windows) Option (Mac) while dragging the mask to each of the other layers.

On the other hand, if you simply need to move a mask to one other layer, just drag the mask to that layer.

#79 Modifying a Layer Mask

Modifying layer masks is easy and rewarding. If you know how to choose a color in the Toolbox and paint with the Brush tool, you know how to modify a layer mask—that's all it initially takes!

To modify a layer mask:

1. In the Layers panel, click the layer mask thumbnail (located to the right of the layer icon). Once you have clicked it, a bracketed border appears around the mask thumbnail indicating it is active (**Figure 79a**).

Figure 79a A border appears around an active layer mask.

2. Choose an editing or painting tool.

3. Paint or fill with one of the following:

   • White to reveal the layer contents.

   • Black to conceal the layer contents.

   • Gray to make the layer contents partially visible. Darker grays conceal more; lighter grays reveal more.

Figure 79b, a fun photograph of my youngest daughter, is a good example of an image in which modifying a layer mask is the best way to improve it.

Figure 79b This image would benefit from an enhancement that involves sharpening and masking to sharpen just the eyes.

Link and Unlink a Layer Mask

By default, a layer is linked to its layer mask. The link is identified in the Layers panel by a small link icon that appears between the thumbnails in the Layers panel. Typically, when you create a layer mask, it is best to leave the layer and the layer mask linked. Then if you move either one using the Move tool, the layer and its mask move together.

However, if you need to move the layer and its mask independently, click the link icon to unlink them. To reestablish the link, click in the space between the layer and its mask.

To sharpen the eyes in the image, I first copied the Background layer and then applied the Smart Sharpening filter (see Chapter 13, "Sharpening"), which sharpens the entire image. Then I created a mask filled with black to conceal the sharpening (Alt-click [Windows] Option-click [Mac] the Add a Pixel Mask icon). I chose the Brush tool and then chose white as the foreground color (click the Foreground Color box in the Toolbox and choose white from the Color Picker). I painted on the eyes with the Brush tool, adding white to the layer mask and revealing the sharpened layer beneath.

The eyes ended up being much sharper, making the overall image much more compelling.

For more advanced layer mask controls, navigate to the Masks panel. To open the Masks panel (**Figure 79c**), click on the Masks panel tab. Use these essential controls as follows:

- Move the **Density** slider to control the opacity of the mask. In other words, the Density slider allows you to lower the intensity of what it blocks. A lower percentage means more of the underlying layer is visible.

- Modify the **Feather** slider to create a softer transition between the masked and unmasked areas.

(continued on next page)

Layer Masking Shortcuts

To become more efficient at masking, try the following shortcuts:

- Shift-click on the layer mask thumbnail to toggle the mask on and off.

- Alt-click (Windows) Option-click (Mac) the layer mask thumbnail to toggle between displaying the image and displaying the mask in the main document window.

- Shift + Alt-click (Windows) Shift + Option-click (Mac) the layer mask thumbnail to toggle between showing the mask in red superimposed on the image and the actual image.

- Click the **Mask Edge** button to open the Refine Edges dialog box, which will help you improve the edge areas of the mask (for more information on Refine Edges see #54).

- Click the **Color Range** button to open the Color Range dialog box; make a selection and then a mask based on color (for more information on Color Range see #55).

- Click **Invert** to reverse the mask so that black becomes white and white becomes black.

Figure 79c The Masks panel is a wonderful new addition to Photoshop CS4. Use this panel to work on your masks in many ways.

Tip
Because layer masking is integral to your work in Photoshop, be sure to look for the free tutorial video on http://tv.adobe.com.

#80 Removing Color Using a Mask

Sometimes you need to remove color from an image to enhance it. Using a layer mask to accomplish this gives you increased control and flexibility.

Although this how-to is very specific, keep in mind that the process and techniques described here are actually more important than the project. In other words, what you learn in this how-to can be applied to a wide variety of image-enhancement scenarios.

This particular masking technique is very easy to understand, and as a result, it often helps people learn how masks actually work. Many of my photography students finally experience the "masking a-ha moment" when they practice removing color in this way.

For your first try at removing color using a layer mask, choose an image from which it's simple to remove color. In this example, I'm using an image of an orange California poppy against an out-of-focus purple and green background of wildflowers. Let's focus on removing all the color in the image except for the main object. So, in the example, the poppy color will remain.

To remove color using a layer mask:

1. Click the Adjustment Layer icon at the bottom of the Layers panel and choose Hue/Saturation from the menu (**Figure 80a**). A Hue/Saturation adjustment layer is added to the image.

Figure 80a Create an adjustment layer above the image layer.

(continued on next page)

Adding Color Using a Mask

Sometimes an effect that's even more interesting than removing color is to add color using a mask. For example, in a portrait in which the model has blue eyes, you might want to enhance the blue eye color. To do this, you would execute the same steps as you would to remove color except you'd substitute the following:

1. In the Hue/Saturation dialog box, increase the saturation by 5 to 10 points and click OK.

2. Fill the mask with black to conceal the color saturation.

3. Using the Brush tool, paint with white on the eyes to reveal the more saturated layer.

2. In the Hue/Saturation dialog box, decrease the saturation by 100 points to remove all the color. Click OK. The image is now in grayscale.

By default, when you create an adjustment layer, a layer mask filled with white is automatically created along with it. Thus, the entirety of the adjustment is revealed.

3. Click the mask thumbnail to activate the mask. With the Brush tool, paint with black on the area that you want to restore to full color (**Figure 80b**).

Black to conceal desaturation on the flower

Adjustment Layer icon

Figure 80b The area that is painted with black on the Hue/Saturation adjustment layer mask conceals the desaturation, thus allowing the original color to show through the mask.

After you have finished painting with black on the mask, the image is complete. In the example, the color of the California poppy stands out boldly from the gray background. Because this book isn't printed in color, you'll need to use your imagination to fully visualize the effect.

#81 Blending Images Using a Mask

One of the more common uses of masking is to blend multiple images together to create a photographic collage. The advantage of using masking for this purpose is that you can blend without actually deleting pixels.

To blend images using a mask:

1. Open multiple images in Photoshop.

2. Choose the Move tool.

3. Drag the images into one document. Each image will occupy a separate layer. **Figure 81a** uses four images of a very happy child.

Figure 81a Multiple images dragged into one Photoshop document. I added a white border to each image to highlight the overlapping edges. Even without these borders, the images would blend well together.

4. Use the Move tool to position the images.

5. Select an image layer and click the Add a Pixel Mask icon in the Layers panel.

6. Repeat step 5 for each image layer.

7. Choose the Brush tool; then in the options bar, choose a brush with soft edges.

(continued on next page)

8. Paint around the edges of each of the images to soften their sharp edges. This helps to blend the layers into a unified image (**Figure 81b**).

Masks that were created with the Brush tool to soften edges and blend images together

Figure 81b By creating a mask on each image, you can soften the edges and blend the images together.

When you are finished, the final image should be a more compelling and cohesive collage as a result of the masking (**Figure 81c**).

Figure 81c Each image in the final photographic collage of my daughter has softer edges. Ultimately, the softness of the edges better blends the photos together.

#82 Using Quick Mask

If you enjoy being able to make "selections" by painting on a layer mask, you will really like using Quick Mask mode. As the name implies, this mode gives you the ability to make a mask quickly. Think of Quick Mask as a temporary way to make a painted or mask-based selection.

Here's how to use Quick Mask mode:

1. Do one of the following:

   • Select part of the image that you want to change—you will then refine the selection in Quick Mask mode.

   • If you want to wait until you're in Quick Mask mode before creating the selection, do nothing.

2. Click the Quick Mask icon in the Toolbox (**Figure 82a**) or press the Q key. If you have an active selection, a red color overlays the unselected (protected) parts of the image, signifying that Quick Mask mode is enabled. The red color represents the mask.

Quick Mask icon

Figure 82a Click the Quick Mask icon to enter Quick Mask mode.

3. To edit the mask, paint with the Brush tool. Paint with white to select more of an image (the color overlay is removed from areas painted with white). To deselect areas, paint over them using black.

4. When you are finished painting, exit Quick Mask mode by clicking the Quick Mask icon in the Toolbox or by pressing the Q key.

   After exiting Quick Mask mode, the clear (non-red) area will turn into a selection.

(continued on next page)

Painting with Gray

While in Quick Mask mode, painting with gray creates a semitransparent area, which can be helpful when you need to soften or feather a selection edge.

Creating a Permanent Layer Mask

Most of the time you'll want to convert the temporary selection you created using Quick Mask mode into a permanent layer mask. Otherwise, you will lose the Quick Mask mode selection. To create a permanent mask, exit Quick Mask mode, and then click the Add a Pixel Mask icon on the Layers panel.

For more Quick Mask options, double-click the Quick Mask icon in the Toolbox to open the Quick Mask Options dialog box (**Figure 82b**).

Figure 82b Double-click the Quick Mask icon to open the Quick Mask Options dialog box.

CHAPTER ELEVEN

Retouching Portraits

Last year I had the opportunity to photograph one of the top-ranked tri-athletes in the world. My assignment was to create a telling portrait for a major publication. When I started planning the shot, my first thought was, how do I capture the essence of this athlete and make him look good?

When you stop to think about it, much of a photographer's work with portrait photography is to use the specific environments, lighting, perspectives, and Photoshop techniques that help make a subject look good. The important fact to keep in mind is that different genres of photography require different types of retouching. You do not simply retouch an image because you can. Rather, you retouch to fit the parameters of the genre and the goal of the image. For example, the level of skin smoothing you might do varies, depending on whether the subject is a high-end fashion model or a rural farmer.

This chapter presents a few basic and essential retouching skills that you can apply to many of your images. But first it is important to note that this chapter was intentionally placed near the end of the book because it utilizes many of the skills you learned in previous chapters. For example, some of the retouching techniques require a basic understanding of blending modes and masking. If you haven't flipped through these chapters yet, be sure to do so before you begin. This will help you make higher-quality improvements to your images.

#83 Reducing Red Eye

Red eye, which is a result of the camera flash reflecting off the subject's retina, can ruin an image. Not to worry, Photoshop has a tool dedicated to quickly and easily fix this problem.

To remove red eye using Photoshop:

1. Choose the Red Eye tool from the Toolbox (**Figure 83a**).

Figure 83a By default, the Red Eye tool is hidden behind the Spot Healing Brush tool.

2. Select the eye using one of the following techniques:

- Click the center of the eye to select it.
- Drag a rectangle around the eye to select it. It is best to create a rectangle that is slightly bigger than the iris (**Figure 83b**).

Figure 83b The eye selected with the Red Eye tool.

3. Release the mouse button; the red is removed automatically.

4. In the options bar, adjust the Pupil Size and Darken Amount values to fine-tune the correction (**Figure 83c**). Pupil Size increases or decreases the area affected by the Red Eye tool. Darken Amount sets the darkness of the correction.

5. Repeat these steps for the other eye(s) in the image that needs correcting.

Figure 83c Adjust the values for Pupil Size and Darken Amount in the options bar to fine-tune the red eye removal.

Note

To reduce red eye using Adobe Camera Raw, see #37.

What Causes Red Eye?

Red eye is caused by a reflection of the camera flash in the subject's retina. Red eye occurs most frequently (but is not limited to) the increased size of the subject's retina because of darkened conditions. Most cameras today come equipped with a red-eye reduction flash setting. However, this feature doesn't always do the trick, especially when using point-and-shoot cameras that have short distances between their lenses and their flashbulbs.

#**84** Retouching Blemishes

When you clean your house, it makes more sense to dust the furniture and bookcase before you vacuum the floor than it does to do it the other way around—vacuuming before you dust. The same is true with digital retouching. It makes more sense to remove blemishes and distractions, and then work on other enhancements like wrinkle reduction.

Removing blemishes

Let's begin by learning how to reduce blemishes and distracting elements in an image. One of the tools you'll use is the Healing Brush tool. The Healing Brush tool works much like the Retouching tool in the Camera Raw plug-in that was discussed in #38. It lets you sample pixels from a relatively unblemished part of the image (known as the sample point) and blend those pixels over the part of the image you're trying to repair.

Most professional retouchers create a retouching "road map" before they begin (**Figure 84a**). This involves creating a new layer and then circling any distracting elements. A road map such as this will help you determine what needs to be retouched.

Figure 84a Before you begin retouching, create a new layer and circle the distracting elements.

Once you have your road map, you can begin to remove the rough patches:

1. Create a new layer for each type of blemish. In **Figure 84b**, the created layers include Back Drop, Nose, and Zipper.

Figure 84b Create a separate layer for each type of blemish.

2. Select the layer where you want to begin your corrections.

3. Choose the Healing Brush tool. Then in the options bar, choose All Layers from the Sample menu (**Figure 84c**).

Figure 84c When healing to separate layers, be sure to choose All Layers from the Sample menu in the options bar.

4. Alt-click (Windows) Option-click (Mac) the location where you want to set the sample point; in other words, the spot from which you want to borrow sample pixels to repair the image.

5. Paint with the Healing Brush and Clone Stamp tools to remove the blemishes.

Tip

Using both the Healing Brush and the Clone Stamp tools often produces better results than if you just use one tool or the other.

Advanced Retouching

Here is a professional portrait-retouching secret that is worth its weight in gold: Most professional retouching is actually done using the Clone Stamp tool and different blending modes. This technique can be a bit trickier than using the Healing Brush tool, but the potential for much more rewarding results is worth it.

1. Choose the Clone Stamp tool.

2. Choose these options from the options bar:

   • To remove dark blemishes, choose the Lighten blending mode. The cloning will affect only the darker pixels. Then choose a low opacity.

   • To remove light blemishes, select the Multiply or Darken blending mode. The cloning will affect only the lighter pixels. Then choose a low opacity.

3. Create a new layer for each type of blemish, such as freckles, skin blemishes, and so on.

4. Paint over the blemish using the Clone Stamp tool.

Reducing wrinkles

Wrinkles can add a lot of character to a face. So it's very important to keep in mind that the goal is not to completely remove wrinkles, lest you end up practicing "fake-looking" photography. Rather, the goal is to reduce the intensity of the shadows as a way to enhance the image.

Let's use the face of the woman in **Figure 84d** as an example.

Figure 84d This image would benefit from a little wrinkle reduction around the corners of the eyes.

1. Create a new layer for each area that you want to touch up, such as the left or right corners of the eyes or the forehead (**Figure 84e**).

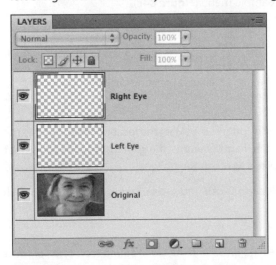

Figure 84e Create new layers for each area to be retouched.

2. Set the sample area that you want to copy pixels from by choosing the Healing Brush tool and Alt-clicking (Windows) Option-clicking (Mac) the area just below the wrinkles. You want a sample source that is "clean" and free of blemishes (**Figure 84f**).

Figure 84f Alt-click (Windows) Option-click (Mac) to set the sample area on a patch of skin that does not have wrinkles.

3. Paint the wrinkled area with the Healing Brush (**Figure 84g**). Be careful to not paint over high contrast or dark areas like eyelashes, eyebrows, and hair.

Figure 84g Wrinkles have been removed with the Healing Brush.

(continued on next page)

4. To keep the image from looking unnatural, lower the opacity of the layer on which you painted to bring back some of the wrinkles and character (**Figure 84h**).

Figure 84h The final image with Left and Right Eye layers set to a lower opacity. The final result is not a complete wrinkle removal but rather a smoothing of the wrinkles.

#85 Smoothing Skin

If you look closely at skin, it is anything but smooth and consistent. Instead, the tone, structure, and texture in even just a small area of skin can be very complex.

To create a more flattering portrait, try practicing the comprehensive set of skin-smoothing instructions in this how-to. It involves four processes:

- Setting up the image

- Creating a mask and applying a blur

- Copying the mask to a Texture layer

- Adding some texture

This is an advanced technique, so put on your thinking cap, fasten your seat belt, and get ready for a wild ride!

Setting up the image

To begin the process of smoothing skin in a photograph, add two layers to your original image by clicking the Background and pressing Ctrl + J (Windows) Command + J (Mac) twice. Double-click the Background to open the New Layer dialog box and name it Original (this converts it into a real layer). Then rename the other layers from top to bottom: Texture and Gaussian (**Figure 85a**).

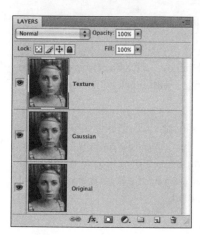

Figure 85a The layer stack for this skin-smoothing project.

Next, click the Eye icon to hide the Texture layer.

Applying the blur

To apply a blur to smooth the skin:

1. Select the Gaussian layer and choose Filter > Blur > Gaussian Blur.

2. In the Gaussian Blur dialog box that appears, drag the Radius slider to set the amount of Gaussian Blur so that the image appears to be behind a piece of slightly frosted glass. The actual amount will vary depending on the image resolution. For starters, try an amount between 3 and 5. Click OK (**Figure 85b**).

Figure 85b Apply the Gaussian Blur filter until the image is blurred but still recognizable.

3. Alt-click (Windows) Option-click (Mac) the Add a Pixel Mask icon in the Layers panel. This creates a mask filled with black, which conceals the Gaussian Blur effect.

4. Choose the Brush tool, select white in the Color Picker, and then lower the opacity (for starters try 70%). Next, begin to paint with white on the areas of skin that need softening. Be careful not to paint on the lips, eyes, eyebrows, hair, and so on. Painting on the layer mask with white reveals the blurred image (**Figure 85c**).

Figure 85c A layer mask hides the Gaussian layer except where skin is exposed.

5. Make the Original and Gaussian layers visible by clicking their Eye icons. In the options bar, lower the opacity of the Gaussian layer to approximately 50% or whatever percentage looks best. A good way to find the best value is to modify the opacity, look away or close your eyes, and then look back to see if it still looks okay.

Tip
Another great filter for blurring the skin is Surface Blur. To use this filter, simply follow the preceding steps except use Surface Blur instead of Gaussian Blur.

Copying the mask
Now you need to copy this mask to the Texture layer. Alt-drag (Windows) Option-drag (Mac) the mask from the Gaussian layer to the Texture layer. This applies a copy of the mask you just created to the Texture layer (**Figure 85d**).

(continued on next page)

Figure 85d The mask from the Gaussian layer is duplicated and added to the Texture layer.

Adding texture

Without some added texture, the blurred image you just created will look too soft. Even the smoothest skin has some texture, so let's add some using the High Pass filter.

1. Click the Eye icon to make the Texture layer visible.

2. Select the Texture layer and remove the color by choosing Image > Adjustments > Desaturate.

3. Select Filter > Other > High Pass.

4. In the High Pass dialog box, increase the Radius setting until you see what looks like a white and gray drawing in the High Pass filter preview. While the Radius amount you specify is largely based on the image's resolution, you should still be able to see the shape of the image in the preview window (**Figure 85e**).

Figure 85e In the High Pass dialog box, increase the Radius setting until the image looks similar to the image here.

5. Click OK to apply the High Pass filter.

6. Change the blending mode of the Texture layer to Soft Light.

7. Decrease the layer opacity to approximately 40% (again, the actual amount is contingent upon image resolution).

Tip
If at the end of these steps you find that the skin smoothing isn't ideal, don't worry. I typically find that it is necessary to go back to make some minor adjustments to the masks and layer opacities once I am able to see the cumulative effect.

#86 Improving Eyes

In a portrait, the first aspect of the image that draws your attention is the human eye. Some even go so far to say that the eyes are the most important aspect of an image. Therefore, it's definitely worthwhile to learn how to help the viewer focus in on the eyes. This how-to shows you three eye-enhancing techniques that use curves and the Smart Sharpen filter.

Brightening using curves

1. Make a selection of the eyes using the Lasso or Elliptical Marquee tool. Later you'll turn this selection into a mask on an adjustment layer (**Figure 86a**).

Figure 86a Create a rough selection of the eyes using one of the selection tools.

2. In the Layers panel, click the Add Adjustment/Fill Layer icon and choose Curves.

3. In the Curves dialog box that appears, click the middle of the curve and drag up to brighten the eyes (**Figure 86b**).

Figure 86b Use a Curves adjustment layer to brighten the eyes.

4. Paint with a soft-edged brush on the Curves layer mask so that the brightening is limited to the irises.

   Enjoy the final results (**Figure 86c**).

Figure 86c The eyes have been brightened.

Adding sparkle using the Smart Sharpen filter

1. Select the iris of the eye using the Lasso or Elliptical Marquee tool.

2. Press Ctrl + J (Windows) Command + J (Mac) to copy the selection to a new layer.

(continued on next page)

3. Rename the layer Smart Sharpen (**Figure 86d**).

Figure 86d The eyes have been selected and copied to a new layer.

4. Select Filter > Sharpen > Smart Sharpen.

5. In the Smart Sharpen dialog box, increase the sharpening. The Amount and Radius settings you choose will depend on the image resolution; however, try an Amount setting of somewhere near 100% and a Radius setting of between 1 and 3 (**Figure 86e**).

Figure 86e Increase the Amount and Radius settings until you see the desired amount of sharpening.

6. Click OK to apply the Smart Sharpen filter.

7. Lower the opacity of the Smart Sharpen layer and preview the final results (**Figures 86f** and **86g**).

Figure 86f The original image.

Figure 86g The image with eyes sharpened.

#**87** Changing Eye Color

Changing eye color can add a creative twist to an otherwise ordinary image. By making just a small color adjustment to the eyes, the same subject can take on a completely new personality. This how-to presents three techniques for changing eye color.

Using the Color Replacement tool

The advantage of using the Color Replacement tool to enhance eye color is speed—it is the fastest way to change eye color. The disadvantage of using this technique is that it is not as flexible as the other techniques.

1. Select the iris of the eye with the Lasso or Elliptical Marquee tool.

2. Choose Select > Modify > Feather and add a 1-pixel feather to soften the selection edge.

3. Press Ctrl + J (Windows) Command + J (Mac) to copy the selection to a new layer.

4. Rename the layer New Eye Color (**Figure 87a**).

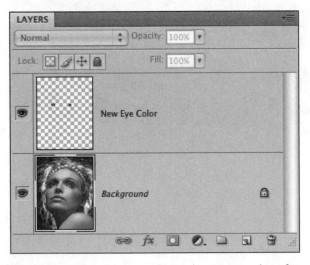

Figure 87a Select the eyes and copy them to a new layer for added flexibility.

5. Choose the Color Replacement tool from the Toolbox (**Figure 87b**).

Figure 87b The Color Replacement tool is hidden behind the Brush tool.

Color Replacement

For more information about the Color Replacement tool, see #72.

6. Click the Foreground Color box on the Toolbox to open the Color Picker and choose a foreground color.

7. Select the New Eye Color layer and paint using the Color Replacement tool. The foreground color replaces the original color in the areas your brush passes over.

Using Hue/Saturation

Using Hue/Saturation to alter eye color gives you more control than the Color Replacement tool. The Hue/Saturation dialog box contains sliders to control hue, saturation, and lightness. Using all three sliders creates the best color.

1. Select the iris of the eye using the Lasso or Elliptical Marquee tool. This selection will later turn into a mask on your adjustment layer.

2. Choose Select > Modify > Feather and add a 1-pixel feather to soften the selection edge.

3. In the Layers panel, click the Add Adjustment/Fill Layer icon and choose Hue/Saturation from the menu.

4. In the Hue/Saturation dialog box, drag the Hue slider to change the eye color (**Figure 87c**).

(continued on next page)

Figure 87c Drag the Hue slider in the Hue/Saturation dialog box to change color.

5. Click OK to apply the color adjustment.

6. Change the opacity of the Hue/Saturation layer to fine-tune the color change.

Applying solid color

The advantage of applying solid color to change the look of the eyes is that it's quick and easy.

1. Select the iris of the eye using the Lasso or Elliptical Marquee tool. This selection will later turn into a mask on the adjustment layer.

2. Choose Select > Modify > Feather and add a 1-pixel feather to soften the selection edge.

3. In the Layers panel, click the Add Adjustment/Fill Layer icon and choose Solid Color.

4. Choose a color from the Color Picker (**Figure 87d**).

Figure 87d Choose a color that you think will look good.

5. Click OK.

Note
Don't evaluate the results of the color you've chosen until you execute the next step.

6. In the Layers panel, change the blending mode of the Color Fill adjustment layer to Color (**Figure 87e**).

(continued on next page)

Blending mode set to color

Color Fill 1

Color fill with a mask to reveal color on eyes

Figure 87e Be sure to change the blending mode to Color.

7. Evaluate the results. If you are unhappy with the color you've chosen, it's easy to change. In the Layers panel, double-click the Color Fill adjustment layer icon to reopen the Color Picker. Choose a new color and click OK.

#**88** Whitening Teeth

Yesterday, I was standing in the line at the grocery store, and someone standing near me pointed to the cover of a magazine and said to me, "Whoa, those teeth are white!" The teeth were so white that they overpowered the photograph. In reality, the problem with natural teeth isn't that they aren't pure white, it is that they are a bit yellow. Thus, the goal here is to brighten and whiten teeth by removing some, but not all, of the yellow.

1. Select the teeth using one of the selection tools, such as the Magnetic Lasso, Lasso, or Quick Selection tool. This selection will later turn into a mask on your adjustment layer.

2. Choose Select > Modify > Feather and add a 2-pixel feather to soften the selection edge (**Figure 88a**).

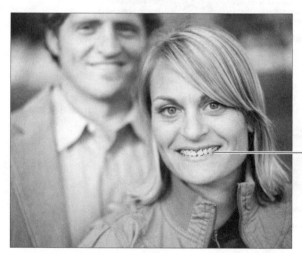

Teeth selected and 2-pixel feather added

Figure 88a The teeth are selected.

3. In the Layers panel, click the Add Adjustment/Fill Layer icon and choose Hue/Saturation from the menu.

4. In the Hue/Saturation dialog box, choose Yellows from the Edit menu.

(continued on next page)

5. Use the Saturation slider to reduce the saturation of the yellows until the yellow is diminished. Don't go too far or the teeth with look gray (**Figure 88b**).

Figure 88b Reduce the saturation of the yellow tones in the image.

6. From the Edit menu, choose Master.

7. Increase the Lightness to approximately 20 points (**Figure 88c**).

Figure 88c Increase the overall lightness of the image.

8. Click OK to apply the teeth-whitening effect.

9. Click in the Hue/Saturation adjustment layer. Press Ctrl + J (Windows) Command+ J (Mac) to duplicate the layer. Change the duplicated layer's blending mode to Soft Light to add a touch of contrast. Lower the opacity to approximately 45% or until the contrast looks good (**Figure 88d**).

Figure 88d Because the teeth have been desaturated and brightened, it is key that you change the duplicated layer's blending mode to ensure that the teeth have a good amount of contrast.

Note
If the effect is too strong using this method, lower the layer opacity in the Layers panel.

CHAPTER TWELVE

Working with Type

Learning how to effectively work with type can set you apart from the typical Photoshop user. People often concentrate on learning how to utilize Photoshop's core strengths for image editing and then overlook the many powerful and creative Photoshop type tools and tricks. Those who take time to learn about type are well rewarded, because they will have the ability to combine image, design, and type with unparalleled possibilities. This chapter will get you up to speed on type essentials and further your progress on becoming a Photoshop expert.

But first, it's worth pointing out that type in Photoshop is vector based. In other words, Photoshop type consists of vector-based outlines—mathematically defined shapes that describe the letters, numbers, and symbols of a typeface. In contrast, the bulk of your work in Photoshop comprises pixel-based bitmap images.

What's the big deal about type being vector based? Vector-based type can be scaled without any degradation of quality. How does this actually work? Photoshop preserves vector-based type outlines and uses them when you scale or resize type, output a PDF or EPS file, print the image to a PostScript printer, or save for the Web or for other devices. All of this empowers you to produce printed or Web-based type with crisp, resolution-independent edges.

#89 Adding Type

Adding type to your document is easy:

1. Choose one of the Type tools in the Toolbox (**Figure 89a**).

Figure 89a The various Type tools all live on the same tile in the Toolbox.

2. In the options bar, choose the font, font size, and type of anti-aliasing you want (**Figure 89b**).

Figure 89b Choose the appropriate Type tool settings in the options bar.

3. Move the cursor over the document window and click to add type. By default, this will create a new type layer (**Figure 89c**). The cursor will change to a blinking horizontal line to signify that you can begin typing.

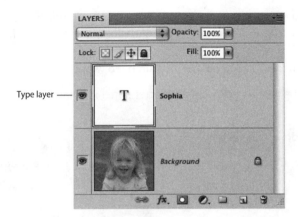

Figure 89c When you use a Type tool, by default it creates a new type layer.

Type layer — Sophia

Background

Not All Text Is Editable

In most typical color modes like RGB, type is completely editable. However, this is not the case in Multichannel, Bitmap, or Indexed Color mode. Because these modes don't support layers, type layers aren't created. As a result, in these modes, type appears in the background as rasterized and uneditable text.

Modifying and Rasterizing Type

Certain type modifications require that you rasterize the type layer. For example, you must first rasterize a type layer before you can apply the Distort filter. When you rasterize type, you turn the type layer into bitmapped artwork, rendering the text uneditable. To rasterize type, choose Layer > Rasterize > Type.

4. Enter the text you want.

5. Press Enter or select another tool in the Toolbox to commit the changes.

Editing a type layer

After you have created a type layer, it can be edited at any time. To edit a type layer, follow these steps:

1. Select the type layer in the Layers panel.

2. Select a Type tool from the Toolbox.

3. Position the cursor over the text field ⟨I⟩ where it will change its appearance from the default cursor to the insertion point cursor I signifying that you can click and select or edit the text.

4. Click to place the insertion point in the text.

5. Select one or more characters you want to edit.

6. Enter text or change the font, font size, and so on.

7. Press Enter to commit the changes.

#90 Customizing Type

The Character panel is a powerful type-customization engine. After you have added type to your document, you can use this panel to give it that extra boost.

You can open the Character panel in a number of ways:

- Choose a Type tool and click the Character panel icon in the options bar [icon].
- Choose Window > Character.
- Expand the Character panel by clicking its icon in the dock (**Figure 90a**).

Figure 90a The Character panel expanded from the dock.

Once the panel is open, you can customize your text. Start by selecting the text you want to modify as described in the previous how-to (#89). Then in the Character panel, choose options for the type (**Figure 90b**). For example, you might alter any of the following:

- **Font.** Choose a different font from the Font menu.
- **Color.** Click the color swatch to open the Color Picker.
- **Leading** or **Tracking.** For either property, choose a value from the menu, or use the up and down arrows to set the value, or edit the value directly in the text box. Press Enter (Windows) Return (Mac) to apply a value.

Figure 90b A guide to the Character panel.

If you are new to typography, the most common (and essential) type modifications are for leading and tracking. Leading (rhymes with wedding) refers to the vertical space between lines of type (**Figure 90c**). Tracking is the loosening or tightening of the spacing between the characters in selected text or an entire block of text (**Figure 90d**).

CREATIVITY IS SEEING
    THE ORDINARY   —— Leading = 24pt
AS EXTRAORDINARY

CREATIVITY IS SEEING
AS EXTRAORDINARY   —— Leading = 9pt

Figure 90c Change the leading to increase or decrease the vertical space between the lines of type.

    CREATIVITY IS SEEING
      THE ORDINARY   —— Tracking = 0
    AS EXTRAORDINARY

CREATIVITY IS SEEING
    THE ORDINARY   —— Tracking = 270
AS EXTRAORDINARY

Figure 90d Change the tracking to increase or decrease the space between the characters.

#91 Adding Creative Type Effects

Creative Type Effects Resource

This how-to only scratches the surface of applying creative type effects. For more inspiration, check out the free Photoshop Creative Type tutorials at www.planetphotoshop. com/category/text.

This how-to focuses on three creative type effects that can increase your type skills and inspire you to be more creative with type in Photoshop.

Warp effects

Warp type effects are really fun because they give you the ability to change the shape, orientation, or perspective of the type. For example, you can make the type warp to fit inside the shape of a flag or arc the type up or down. These effects are most useful when you are interested in adding creative type to your document.

1. Choose a Type tool from the Toolbox.

2. Add type to your document (**Figure 91a**).

ANNIKA KAI ORWIG

Figure 91a Default type without warp effects.

3. Select a type layer in the Layers panel.

4. Click the Create Warped Text icon ![icon] in the options bar. The Warp Text dialog box opens.

5. Choose a warp style from the Style menu (**Figure 91b**).

Figure 91b In this case, I chose the Arc style.

6. In the Warp Text dialog box, drag the sliders to change the Bend and Horizontal and/or Vertical Distortion settings.

7. Click OK to apply the warp effect (**Figure 91c**).

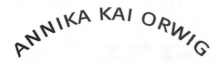

Figure 91c The final results of the Arc warp style.

Drop shadow

A drop shadow is a shadow that appears behind the text. Adding a drop shadow to type can potentially add dimension and visual interest to the type.

1. With any tool chosen, select a type layer in the Layers panel.

2. Choose Layer > Layer Style > Drop Shadow.

3. In the Layer Style dialog box, modify the controls in the Structure and Quality areas (**Figure 91d**).

Figure 91d Use these controls to fine-tune the Drop Shadow effect.

(continued on next page)

Undoing a Warp Effect

To undo a warp effect, follow steps 1 through 3, and then choose None from the menu. This will completely remove the warp effect.

4. Click OK to apply the effect.

5. The Drop Shadow effect will appear in the Layers panel below the type layer (**Figure 91e**). Click the eye icon to hide or show the effect. Double-click the word *Drop Shadow* to reopen the Layer Style dialog box to change the drop shadow controls.

Drop Shadow

Layer Style Effects icon

Layer Style Effect

Figure 91e The Drop Shadow effect and the Layers panel showing the Drop Shadow effect listed under the type layer to which it is applied.

Fill type with an image

Type usually is filled with a solid color or gradient. However, there are times when you need to go beyond the typical. Here I show you how to fill type with an image by applying a clipping mask:

1. Create a document with a type layer and an image layer (**Figure 91f**).

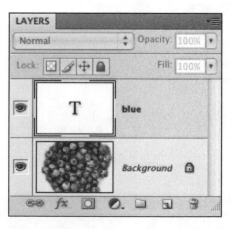

Figure 91f A document with an image of blueberries and a type layer.

2. If the image is the Background, double-click it to convert it to a regular layer and give it a name.

3. Reposition the layers by dragging so that the image layer is on top of the type layer (**Figure 91g**).

Figure 91g The image layer has been restacked above the type layer.

4. Select the top layer. Choose Layer > Create Clipping Mask. The clipping mask is displayed in the Layers panel (**Figure 91h**).

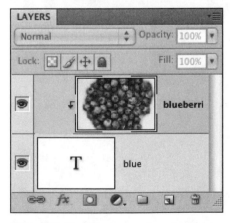

Figure 91h The clipping mask as displayed in the Layers panel.

(continued on next page)

#91: Adding Creative Type Effects

The result of applying a clipping mask is that the text is filled with the image (**Figure 91i**).

Figure 91i The final result: The type is filled with the image of the blueberries.

Tip
After you have filled text with an image, experiment with the text and image layers. Click the image layer and drag it around so that different parts of the image fill the text. Then click the type layer and change the font, font size, and so on.

CHAPTER THIRTEEN

Sharpening Images

There is something incredibly compelling about photographs that are vivid and sharp. It's as if the sharpness draws us in, making us want to look closer. As you strive to create sharp images, you stand on the shoulders of many great photographers, including Ansel Adams, who pioneered and evangelized the idea that precision and sharp focus are fundamental to good photography.

While Ansel's pursuit to capture sharp images was focused on the camera and printing, you now have an even bigger advantage— Photoshop, which provides a number of sharpening filters. This chapter focuses on the most useful of these filters.

Keep in mind that no one sharpening filter is best, and no one sharpening technique works for every image. It's important that you be familiar with and practice using all of them so that you have a broad base of sharpening skills that you can apply, as appropriate, when fine-tuning your images.

It's also important to remember that it's best to incorporate sharpening as the last step in your imaging workflow. Completing all other enhancements, such as retouching, color and tone adjustments, image enhancements, and resizing *before* you sharpen is critical. This approach will deliver the best sharpening results for that particular image size and resolution.

Of course, Ansel was interested in more than just the fundamentals of precision and sharpness. His goal was to create strong and compelling photographs. As he once said, "There's nothing worse than a sharp photograph of a fuzzy concept."

As you learn how to sharpen images in Photoshop, remember not to lose sight of this ultimate goal: to create images that have impact. If you do lose sight and end up oversharpening your images (a predicament common to those who are new to digital imaging), you run the risk of calling attention to the sharpness rather than the actual images.

#92 Using the Unsharp Mask Filter

One of the most useful sharpening tools Photoshop provides is the Unsharp Mask filter. (Yes, the name sounds like it does the opposite of sharpening—it's derived from an old darkroom technique where the name does make sense.) This filter scans the image for areas where pixels whose tonal values differ by a certain quantity (the "threshold," chosen by you) are right next to each other. These areas tend to be edges, and the filter lets you sharpen these edges by increasing the contrast of pixels within those areas. In other words, you lighten the light pixels and darken the dark pixels, and the boundaries between them become more pronounced.

Sharpening an image involves a bit of "give and take." While you want to increase the overall sharpness of the image, you do not want to increase or exaggerate noise or artifacts. Fortunately, the Unsharp Mask filter has controls that help you specify an ideal amount of sharpening without degrading the overall image quality. Use this filter, as opposed to the others, when you're interested in making precise sharpening improvements to your image.

To use the Unsharp Mask filter:

1. Select the layer you want to sharpen.

2. Choose Filter > Sharpen > Unsharp Mask. The Unsharp Mask dialog box appears (**Figure 92a**).

Figure 92a The Unsharp Mask dialog box.

3. Select the Preview option and adjust the Amount using the slider or enter a percentage.

The Amount setting controls the overall intensity of the sharpening. The value you specify determines how much to increase the contrast of the pixels. The actual Amount depends on your image's size and resolution. For medium- to high-resolution images, try an Amount of 100%. For higher-resolution images, try a higher percentage.

4. Adjust the Radius setting, which controls the "reach" of the sharpening. If you are sharpening any edge, for instance, the Radius setting defines how far the sharpening will extend on either side of this line. In more specific terms, the setting determines the number of pixels surrounding the edge pixels that will be affected.

The greater the Radius value, the wider the edge effects will be, and the more obvious the sharpening. So your Radius amount will typically be low. For example, for images destined for Web pages, try a Radius between .1 and .3. For high-resolution print images, try a radius between 1 and 3.

5. Adjust the Threshold setting. This setting "saves the day" by limiting the extent of your sharpening. When the filter evaluates a pixel for sharpening, it compares its tonal value with that of its neighbors. If the difference is less than the Threshold setting, nothing happens. If the difference is greater, the contrast between the pixel and the ones around it is increased.

When the Threshold value is set to 0 (the default setting), if there's any difference at all between tonal values, sharpening is applied. This means that even tiny fluctuations in tone, such as image noise and film grain, will be exaggerated. Raising the value above 0 means that only more defined features, such as edges with contrast, will be sharpened, whereas broad areas of near-uniform texture, like skin and sky, will be protected from sharpening.

The appropriate setting will vary, depending on the nature of the image. The more detail there is, the lower the setting. For starters, try a value between 2 and 20. Images with a lot of detail usually require a low setting; use higher settings for images with less detail (like portraits).

(continued on next page)

#92: Using the Unsharp Mask Filter

Best Practices

When using the Unsharp Mask filter, it is often difficult to see the results in the image. Follow these steps to improve your sharpening:

- The Unsharp Mask dialog box often obscures important parts of the image in the document window. Therefore, it's important to reposition the dialog box so that you can effectively preview the sharpening. This may seem obvious, but it's easy to forget.

- Clicking the preview image in the dialog box and holding down the mouse shows you the preview without the sharpening. Releasing the mouse button lets you see the preview with the sharpening applied. Toggling back and forth lets you more easily notice the effects of the sharpening.

- In the dialog box, click and drag the preview to see different parts of the image. You can also click the plus (+) or minus (−) buttons under the preview image to zoom in or out.

6. When your sharpening appears to look its best, click OK to apply the sharpening.

Figure 92b shows the before and after versions of a sharpening project.

Before applying Unsharp Mask · · · · · · · · · After applying Unsharp Mask

Figure 92b The image on the right is stronger because it has been sharpened with the Unsharp Mask filter.

Tip
To accurately evaluate and dial in the appropriate amount of sharpening, always make sure you're looking at the image in the document window at 100%.

Tip
If after applying the Unsharp Mask filter, you notice that noise has become exaggerated or that bright colors appear overly saturated, choose Edit > Fade Unsharp Mask, and then choose Luminosity from the Mode menu. This reduces potential color problems caused by the Unsharp Mask filter.

Original

Oversharpened

——— Halo around edges reveals
Sharpening is too High

Figure 92c The lower image has been
oversharpened and the result is an overexaggerated
amount of edge contrast and brightness. It is as if the
edges glow or have a halo.

The Halo Effect

Oversharpening can produce a halo effect around the edges of a subject that
has been sharpened (**Figure 92c**). Look closely at your image, and if you see
the halo effect, reduce sharpening.

#93 Using the Smart Sharpen Filter

The Smart Sharpen filter, as its name implies, seems almost as if it is truly smart. It is more powerful than the Unsharp Mask filter (#92) with sharpening controls that Unsharp Mask doesn't share and can provide better results. So why not always use Smart Sharpen instead of Unsharp Mask? The process of sharpening an image with Smart Sharpen is slightly slower than with Unsharp Mask. But some things, like the high-quality results of Smart Sharpen, are worth the wait.

To use the Smart Sharpen filter:

1. Select the layer you want to sharpen.

2. Choose Filter > Sharpen > Smart Sharpen to open the Smart Sharpen dialog box (**Figure 93a**).

Click in the preview window to see the before/after or select/deselect the Preview check box

Select Advanced for more options

Use the Advanced Shadow/Highlight tabs to remove a halo effect

Choose the type of sharpening: Gaussan, Lens, or Motion

Select More Accurate for sharpening very small details

Click "+" or "–" icons to zoom in/out

Figure 93a The Smart Sharpen dialog box.

3. From the Remove menu, choose the mode of sharpening you want:

   - **Gaussian Blur** sharpens identically to the Unsharp Mask filter.

   - **Lens Blur** is the best choice in the group because it allows you to sharpen typical optical lens blurring. It provides finer sharpening of detail and does a better job of reducing sharpening halos than the Gaussian Blur setting.

   - **Motion Blur** works best when you want to remove small amounts of motion blur that resulted from camera movement. Click the wheel to the right of the Angle field to set the direction of the motion that needs to be removed.

4. Adjust the Amount and Radius controls, which work just like their counterparts in the Unsharp Mask dialog box (see #92), so that the sharpening looks best.

5. Click OK to apply the sharpening.

Tip
Choose the More Accurate option when sharpening images with very small details.

Figure 93b shows the result of using the Smart Sharpen filter. Edges are crisper, especially boundaries between contrasting areas.

Where's the Threshold Slider?

The Threshold slider plays an integral role in the Unsharpen Mask filter, but as you may have noticed, Smart Sharpen does not have a Threshold setting. Does this make Smart Sharpen inferior to the Unsharp Mask filter? Definitely not! The threshold algorithm is built into Smart Sharpen and is automatically applied—that's one of the reasons it's so smart!

Figure 93b On the left before sharpening. On the right after using Smart Sharpen.

When you look closely, you will notice the improved details on the building and trees.

Advanced sharpening

If you notice strong, dark, or light sharpening halos after you have doctored your image, you can reduce them for optimal sharpening using the more advanced controls in the Smart Sharpen dialog box. Select the

Advanced radio button in the Smart Sharpen dialog box to gain access to the Shadow and Highlight tabs (**Figure 93c**). On these tabs, you can adjust the following:

- The **Fade Amount** slider controls the overall amount of sharpening in the highlights or shadows. Choose a higher value to reduce the overall sharpening in the shadows or highlights.

- The **Tonal Width** slider limits the sharpening to specific tonal regions of the image. For example, if you choose a lower Tonal Width in the Shadow or Highlight tabs, the sharpening will be limited to the respective tones. On the Shadow tab, it limits sharpening of the darker tones. On the Highlight tab, it limits sharpening to the brighter tones. A higher value set on either tab expands sharpening to a wider range of tones.

- The **Radius** slider works like its equivalent in the Unsharp Mask dialog box and controls the size of the area around each pixel taken into account by the filter. Moving the slider to the left specifies a smaller area, and moving it to the right specifies a larger area.

Figure 93c Fine-tune the sharpening of the dark and light areas using the Shadow and Highlight tabs. These tabs are especially effective at removing the halo effect.

Tip

The Fade Amount slider often is the only slider you will need to effectively remove halos. Try that slider first. After you have adjusted the Fade Amount slider, experiment with the Tonal Width and Radius sliders to fine-tune your adjustment.

#94 Using High Pass Sharpening

High pass sharpening is an advanced sharpening technique that is easy to learn and apply. I have found this technique to be especially helpful for visual learners who like to see how the sharpening is being applied in a step-by-step fashion.

By way of introduction, this technique uses the High Pass filter, which was originally created for extracting line art and large black-and-white areas from scanned images. However, let's be creative and use this filter to generate a grayscale image, which retains edge details and removes low-frequency detail. This grayscale image is exactly what you'll use to sharpen images. You will find this sharpening technique helpful when you have an image with strong edges that need to be sharpened.

To apply high pass sharpening:

1. Copy the Background layer by choosing Layer > Duplicate Layer. Name the duplicate layer High Pass (**Figure 94a**).

Figure 94a To apply high pass sharpening, you need to duplicate the Background layer.

2. Choose Filter > Other > High Pass.

3. In the High Pass dialog box, set the Radius to a low value (**Figure 94b**). The exact amount will vary based on the image size and resolution. Try a low filter setting of 1.0. The level of grayscale in your image should look something like the one in the preview window of Figure 94b.

(continued on next page)

Figure 94b When applying the High Pass filter, modify the Radius slider so that you can see a grayscale image with edge detail, as shown here.

4. Click OK to apply the filter.

5. Change the blending mode of the High Pass layer to Soft Light (or Hard Light for a stronger sharpening effect). Lower the Opacity to fine-tune the amount of sharpening. Typically, the Opacity amount will be below 50% (**Figure 94c**).

Figure 94c To apply the sharpening, be sure to change the blending mode to Soft Light. To fine-tune sharpening, lower the Opacity setting.

#95 Sharpening Selectively

In my opinion, learning how to selectively sharpen an image is one of the most essential skills for any Photoshop user regardless of his or her experience. Why? Because this technique is based on a core photographic truth: Viewers are attracted to sharpness in an image. Therefore, it is not always best to sharpen everything; sharpening just the key aspects of an image will have more impact. And that's exactly what you'll learn how to do in this how-to. Selective sharpening is a technique that is easy to apply and master.

To apply selective sharpening:

1. Duplicate the Background layer by selecting it and then choosing Layer > Duplicate.

2. Name the duplicate layer Sharpening (**Figure 95a**).

Figure 95a To apply selective sharpening, you first need to duplicate the Background layer. In this case, I have named the duplicate layer Sharpening.

3. Apply sharpening using one of the techniques presented in this chapter.

4. Alt-click (Windows) Option-click (Mac) the Add a Layer Mask icon to add a layer mask filled with black to the Sharpening layer. The layer mask thus created will hide all the sharpening (**Figure 95b**). (For more on masking, see Chapter 10, "Masking.")

(continued on next page)

More on Photography and Selective Sharpening

Photographers know the truth that viewers are attracted to sharpness. Thus, they create images that direct the viewer's eye to what is important.

For example, a common portrait technique is to create an image so that the person's eyes and face are in focus, but the background is out of focus. As a result, the viewer knows where to look, and the image is flattering. In contrast, if everything was in focus, the viewer wouldn't know what to look at, and the background would become distracting.

Therefore, it is helpful to learn how to sharpen key elements of an image so that you direct the viewer's eye away from distraction and toward what is most important in an image.

Fill layer mask with black to conceal sharpening

Figure 95b Create a layer mask that is filled with black to conceal the sharpening.

5. Choose the Brush tool and select a soft brush.

6. Choose white as the foreground color.

7. Paint on the parts of the image you want to sharpen. White will be added to the layer mask, revealing the Sharpening layer below (**Figure 95c**).

Paint white on layer mask to reveal sharpening of the area of the image that is in focus

Figure 95c Because this portrait has a shallow depth of field, I have selectively sharpened the parts of the image that are in focus. Thus, I have painted with white on the face and the surrounding areas that are in focus.

8. If needed, change the layer opacity setting to decrease the sharpening amount.

9. Click the Eye icon on the Sharpening layer to show or hide the sharpening to determine the quality of the sharpening.

CHAPTER FOURTEEN

Output

I recently came across a weathered wood box in my parent's attic. The old box caught my eye, so I opened it and discovered hundreds of well-preserved glass plate negatives that were taken in China in 1906. As I carefully looked through these old images, I thought that I absolutely had to make some prints so that others could see these powerful images.

The same can be said about all our images stored on our boxy computers: Viewing them on a computer is wonderful, but there is something more powerful about seeing them in print.

This chapter focuses on the essential skills needed for outputting images from Photoshop to the Web, devices, PDFs, and prints. I like to think of this chapter as the moment the focus shifts from creation to completion. It is in this final stage of outputting our images from Photoshop, where we get to enjoy the fruits of our labor!

#**96** Optimizing Images for the Web

The Web is an incredibly powerful medium for displaying and distributing images. However, high-quality digital image files can be so large that they take too long to download. The solution is to *optimize* (or decrease the file size and dimensions) for Web delivery—to compress them so that they download more quickly but still maintain the highest quality possible. However, optimizing images for the Web can be problematic. If the proper techniques aren't used, most images end up looking drab. This how-to remedies that problem: It shows you the essential techniques for optimizing your images so that they look their best.

Optimizing an image for the Web is a complex process that involves several phases:

1. Resizing

2. Preparing image color and contrast

3. Sharpening

4. Saving for the Web

Resizing the image

Resizing an image correctly can make the difference between having a tack-sharp or less-than-ideal soft Web image.

Before you resize the image, take a moment to consider that you will need to change the pixel dimensions to the appropriate size for the intended output. For example, a typical monitor resolution is 1024 x 768, so the image dimensions will need to be sized down to something less than that. The final size of the image will vary; an appropriate sample image size is 700 x 500.

1. Open the image in Photoshop.

2. Choose Image > Image Size to display the Image Size dialog box (**Figure 96a**).

Figure 96a The Image Size dialog box.

3. Select the appropriate interpolation method from the Resample Image menu at the bottom of the dialog box. If you need to decrease the image dimensions, choose Bicubic Sharper. If you need to increase the image dimensions, choose Bicubic Smoother.

4. Change the settings in the Pixel Dimensions area to the desired height and width, such as 700 x 500. When you change the settings, keep in mind that you are not to force the file to fixed dimensions. All you need to do is change the width or the height, not both. Then, with Constrain Proportions turned on, you will resize the image and keep the aspect ratio safe.

5. Click OK to commit to the image resizing.

Preparing image color and contrast

For an image to look its best on the Web, it's important to assign the proper color profile to it and to boost its contrast and color saturation.

1. Choose Edit > Convert to Profile.

2. In the Convert to Profile dialog box, choose sRGB IEC1966-2.1 from the Profile menu in the Destination Space area (**Figure 96b**).

Figure 96b For images to look their best on the Web, they need to be converted to the sRGB profile.

3. Choose Image > Adjustments > Curves.

4. In the Curves dialog box, choose Medium Contrast (RGB) from the Preset menu. This will add contrast and a bit of color saturation.

5. Choose Image > Adjustments > Hue/Saturation.

6. In the Hue/Saturation dialog box, drag the Saturation slider to the right 5 to 10 points to increase the overall color saturation of the image.

Sharpening

The sharpening that you apply to Web images is unique because the images are relatively small and have a low resolution. As a result, you will want to apply a high amount of sharpening that is very evenly distributed across the image.

To sharpen images effectively:

1. Select the layer to be sharpened.

2. Choose Filter > Sharpen > Smart Sharpen to open the Smart Sharpen dialog box.

3. From the Remove menu, choose what you would like sharpened, such as Lens Blur (see Chapter 13, "Sharpening Images," for a discussion of the options in this dialog box).

4. Set the sharpening controls: The Amount typically needs to be high. Try somewhere between 100% and 150%. The Radius needs to be low; try somewhere between .1 and .3 (**Figure 96c**).

Figure 96c Sharpening for the Web involves setting a high amount of sharpening with a low radius.

5. Click OK to apply the sharpening.

Note

For more details on sharpening, see Chapter 13, "Sharpening Images."

Before you begin the process of Web image optimization, it is worth taking a moment to realize that preparing images for the Web involves compromise. Specifically, you will need to compromise between image display quality and the file size of the image.

It is also critical to realize that the optimization involves decreasing the amount of pixels in an image so that the image size is smaller. The process of reducing pixels can cause image degradation. Thus, it is critical to take certain steps so that the smaller and more optimized image can look its best.

Saving for the Web

1. Choose File > Save for Web & Devices to open the Save for Web & Devices dialog box (**Figure 96d**).

Figure 96d Use the Save for Web & Devices dialog box to achieve the best compromise between file size and image quality for your Web images.

2. Click the Optimized tab to see a full view of the image with the applied optimization settings.

3. On the right side of the dialog box, choose JPEG from the first menu on the left (which lists available optimized file formats), and then choose the image compression quality from the second menu on the left. I recommend High for best results.

4. Click OK to save the optimized JPEG file.

Congratulations, the image is now ready for the Web!

#**97** Creating a Web Gallery

Photoshop's Web Photo Gallery command allows you to easily get your images online. What exactly is a Web photo gallery? It is a freestanding Web site that includes a navigation system, thumbnail images, and full-size images. The best part of the deal is that you can use Photoshop to automatically generate a Web gallery from a set of images.

To make your own Web photo gallery:

1. Open Adobe Bridge.

2. Choose Window > Workspace > Output to open the Output workspace. Click the Web Gallery button in the Output panel (**Figure 97a**).

Figure 97a Use the Output panel to determine the gallery template and style, to refresh the preview, and to preview in the browser.

3. Choose a template from the Template options menu. To preview the template, click the Refresh Preview button.

4. Ctrl-click (Windows) Command-click (Mac) to select the files in the Content panel (**Figure 97b**) you want to use in your gallery.

Figure 97b The Content panel displays all the images in a particular location. Choose all the images or just select few to include in the Web gallery.

(continued on next page)

(continued on next page)

Web Gallery Image Order

When Photoshop creates a Web photo gallery, the images are presented in the order in which they're displayed in Bridge. Therefore, it is best to create a custom image order before you create the gallery. From within Bridge, choose View > Sort > Manually. Then drag and reposition the thumbnails in the Content panel to create a manual or custom image order. Once you have finished ordering the images, proceed to create the Web photo gallery.

Customizing the Web Galleries

Photoshop provides a variety of prebuilt styles for your gallery. These can be selected using the Web Photo Gallery command. However, if you have HTML knowledge, you can create a new style or customize a style by editing a set of HTML template files in another program like Adobe Dreamweaver.

5. Open the Site Info panel (**Figure 97c**) to customize the text.

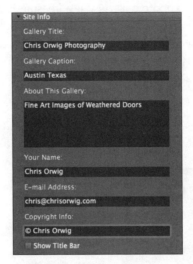

Figure 97c The Site Info panel.

6. Open the Color Palette panel (**Figure 97d**) and choose custom colors.

Figure 97d The Color Palette panel.

7. Open the Appearance panel (**Figure 97e**) to define the image and thumbnail size. In addition, based on the selected template, you can customize other appearance settings.

Figure 97e The Appearance panel.

The Web Gallery is now complete and ready to be uploaded to your Web server.

8. Open the Create Gallery panel (**Figure 97f**) and enter your hosting information. Click the Upload button to transfer the files to the Web.

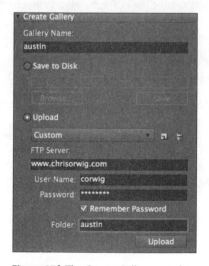

Figure 97f The Create Gallery panel.

The Web Gallery Files

After you have created a Web gallery, you may want to investigate exactly what Photoshop created for you. Open the destination folder where the files are saved. Inside this folder, you will discover subfolders for the HTML, thumbnail JPEGs, and gallery JPEGs. More important, you will find that the first page (or home page) for the gallery is named index.htm. Double-click this file to open it in any Web browser to preview your gallery.

#**98** Saving a PDF

The Output Preview Panel

Even if you are creating a multipage PDF, the Output Preview panel will only display one PDF page. But you can use this preview to customize the layout for all the pages.

Photoshop and Generic PDFs

In Photoshop, you can open and work with two types of PDF files: Photoshop PDF files and generic PDF files. The main difference between Photoshop and generic PDF files is that Photoshop PDF files can contain only a single image, whereas generic PDF files can contain multiple pages and images. When you save PDF files, Photoshop saves them as Photoshop PDF files by default. To save them as generic PDF, in the Save Adobe PDF dialog box, deselect the Preserve Photoshop Editing Capabilities option.

Portable Document Format (PDF) is a flexible, cross-platform, cross-application file format. Created originally by Adobe, PDF is now used by many developers for a variety of different applications. Files saved in PDF format can be shared among various applications on different platforms while retaining their appearance and often their editability.

To save a file in Photoshop PDF format:

1. Open Adobe Bridge.

2. Choose Window > Workspace > Output to open the Output workspace. Click the PDF button in the Output panel (**Figure 98a**).

Figure 98a Use the Output panel to determine the PDF template and to refresh the preview.

3. Ctrl-click (Windows) Command-click (Mac) to select the file(s) in the Content panel you want to use in the PDF.

4. Choose a template option from the Output panel (**Figure 98a**). Click Refresh Preview to view a preview in the Output Preview panel.

5. Change the appearance of the PDF template by customizing the options in the Document, Layout, Overlays, and Watermark areas of the Output panel (**Figure 98b**).

Figure 98b Each PDF template can be completely customized by modifying the controls and settings in these PDF panels.

PDF Presets

Photoshop is equipped with powerful default PDF presets. However, there may be times when your workflow requires customized PDF settings. In these situations, it is advantageous to create and save your own custom presets for reuse in Photoshop or any product in the Adobe Creative Suite.

To create a PDF preset, in the Save Adobe PDF dialog box, set the PDF options you desire and click the Save Preset button.

6. As you make changes to the PDF, be sure to click Refresh Preview to view the changes in the Output Preview panel.

7. For presentations, specify the following options in the Playback panel (**Figure 98c**).

Figure 98c The PDF presentation Playback options.

8. Click Save, or if you'd like to automatically open the PDF in Acrobat after you save it, select View PDF After Save.

#99 Soft-proofing Images

The final step before you print is to view your image as a soft proof. This technique lets you simulate how your image will appear when printed on a particular printer with a particular type of paper. Think of a soft proof as a way to preview the print before the print is actually created.

Soft-proofing may not seem all that important, but in reality it is an essential step toward getting your image to print the way you envision it. Color and tone are created differently on a monitor versus on a printer, which, of course, affects the final print. Color and tone are created via light on a monitor, whereas on a printer they are created via ink that is laid down on a specific type of paper.

The end result of soft-proofing is an increase in color fidelity between the monitor and printer. This extra bit of color accuracy ultimately leads to the creation of a more "color-correct" and compelling image.

To create a soft proof:

1. Make any final modifications to your image.

2. Choose View > Proof Setup > Custom. The Customize Proof Condition dialog box opens.

3. Choose options that correspond to the output condition you want to simulate (**Figure 99**).

Figure 99 Choose the appropriate proof setup options to allow Photoshop to simulate onscreen how the image will appear when it is printed.

Turn Soft-proofing On or Off

You may want to turn soft-proofing on or off. To do this, choose View > Proof Colors. When soft-proofing is on, a check mark appears next to the Proof Colors command, and the name of the proof preset or profile appears at the top of the document window.

Color and Tone Shift

When the soft-proof view is on, you may notice that the colors and tone shift. If this shift is undesirable, make any needed changes to correct the image for those particular output settings.

4. From the Device To Simulate menu, choose the color profile of the device on which you intend to print the proof and which you want to simulate onscreen.

5. Deselect Preserve RGB Numbers (or Preserve CMYK Numbers if your image is CMYK).

6. From the Rendering Intent menu, choose a rendering intent for converting colors to the device you are trying to simulate. Typically, Relative Colorimetric works best for photographs.

7. Select the Black Point Compensation option to preserve important shadow detail when the image is printed. Select this option if you plan to use black point compensation when printing (which is recommended in most situations).

8. If the profile for the device you have chosen to simulate supports the Simulate Paper Color option, you should select it. This option ensures that your soft proof simulates the actual white of the paper.

9. If your profile supports this option, select Simulate Black Ink to simulate the way in which many printers create black, which is using dark gray tones.

10. Click OK to view a soft-proof review.

Soft-proof Comparison

The best way to evaluate a soft proof and to make any needed changes to the image is to first duplicate the original file. Select Image > Duplicate. This gives you two versions of the same image open in Photoshop. Target the original and choose View > Proof Colors. By comparison, you will see a distinct difference between the original and duplicate documents. Once you can see the differences, make any needed changes so that the original (with the soft-proof view on) appears similar to the duplicate (without the soft proof).

#100 Printing Images

There is something magical about creating a print. It is as if printing has the ability to bring your photographic vision to a sense of completion. Creating stunning prints of your images is a complex process, one that's best broken down into four phases:

1. Completing your Photoshop workflow

2. Configuring your print setup options

3. Choosing output and color settings

4. Configuring the printer's Print dialog box

Completing your Photoshop workflow

Make sure that you create a soft proof to simulate how the image will print (see the previous how-to). Make any final color and tone adjustments based on the soft-proof view.

Configuring your print setup options

1. Choose File > Print to open the Print dialog box (**Figure 100a**).

Figure 100a Utilize the Print dialog box to choose the printer and modify page setup and color settings.

2. Set the paper orientation to portrait or landscape by clicking the icons to the right of the image preview.

3. Choose the printer from the Printer menu.

4. Enter the number of copies to print.

5. Click the Page Setup button. In Windows, the Properties dialog box for your specific printer opens; on the Mac, the Page Setup dialog box opens. Choose the size and other characteristics of the paper you intend to print on. The available options depend on your printer, printer drivers, and operating system.

6. The Position and Scaled Print Size areas of the dialog box enable you choose how the image is placed on the paper. Typically, it is better to configure these settings in Photoshop. However, you may find you want to fine-tune or adjust the position and scale of the image in relation to the selected paper size and orientation.

7. Select the Match Print Colors and Show Paper White check box if you want the preview inside the Print dialog box to display a soft-proof color simulation on the particular type of paper you will be using.

8. Select Gamut Warning to reveal which colors are out of gamut.

9. Select the Bounding Box option to view the edges of the image in the preview area. This lets you reposition or scale the image on the print media by dragging.

Choosing output and color settings

1. In the Print dialog box, choose Color Management from the menu on the upper right.

2. Select the Document button to print the image using the color characteristics of the selected printer. (Select Proof to print a simulation of how the image would look if printed on another device.)

3. From the Color Handling menu, choose Photoshop Manages Color.

4. From the Printer Profile menu, choose the profile for your printer and paper. In this case, I have chosen Pro38 PGPP, which is the profile for Epson 3800 Premium Glossy Photo Paper.

5. From the Rendering Intent menu, choose one of the four options. Relative Colorimetric works best for most photographs.

(continued on next page)

Printing on Different Types of Paper

There are a wide array of quality printers and types of paper. In my professional photographic workflow, I have had great success with Epson printers and papers. Whatever type of printer you choose, be sure to experiment with various types of papers. It is typically best to begin experimenting with paper that was created by your brand of printer. I have found some images look great with the extra shine and color saturation that comes with printing on the more typical glossy papers. On the other hand, certain images look more natural on a more specialized textured, velvet, fine art paper.

6. Select Black Point Compensation. This is useful to ensure that the blacks in the image are reproduced accurately to your printer.

7. Click Print. This opens your printer's Print dialog box.

Configuring the printer's Print dialog box

In the Print dialog box, you will need to make a few settings changes. The actual settings options will vary depending on your printer. To demonstrate sample settings, I'm using an Epson 3800 on a Macintosh. (If you're using Windows, you generally access similar controls by clicking the Preferences button in the Print dialog box.)

1. Choose Printer Color Management from the third menu in the Print dialog box and select Off (**Figure 100b**). It is critical that you turn off the printer's color management because you have previously determined that Photoshop will manage the color.

Figure 100b Turning color management off is perhaps the most important of these final steps.

2. From the third menu in the dialog box (the same one you used to choose Color Management), now choose Print Settings, and then choose the appropriate paper type and other settings (**Figure 100c**).

Figure 100c Don't overlook this critical step of selecting the paper type; otherwise, the print quality will not be accurate.

3. Click Print.

Enjoy your final results!

Printing Video Tutorial

Printing photographs is viewed by many as an art. In fact, in photographic circles, there are those who are defined as "print masters."

To gain more mastery over printing, look for the free printing tutorial video on http://tv.adobe.com in the Photoshop section.

Index